MALOU

FRENCH RESISTANCE FIGHTER

MALOU

FRENCH RESISTANCE FIGHTER

MICHÈLE HUPPERT

To my children, Deborah, David, Tommy, Steven,
Leonie & Yasmin

My grandchildren, Rebecca, Judith, Dinah,
Caitlin, Genevieve, Paula, Yehonatan,
Shira, Nechama, Ruth & Halleluya

And the generations to follow

Ruth is the reason you are here

May her life story be your strength and inspiration

RUTH ALTMANN KNEPPEL STEIN
'MALOU'

6 OCTOBER 1913 – 6 JUNE 2007

Ruth was my mother, my dearest friend and my confidante.

A proud Jewess, Zionist and Resistance fighter, Ruth lived her life with great courage, strength and vision. She carried her losses and pain quietly and with great dignity.

Like her own mother, Margaret, Ruth was completely devoted to her family. She was the matriarch of four generations and remained closely connected to each of her grandchildren and great-grandchildren until her final moments.

This book is a tribute to her blessed memory.

The deep void she left within each one of us is now filled with her remarkable story and a formidable legacy to treasure.

Michèle Huppert

Published by Real Film and Publishing
www.realfp.com.au

Text © Michèle Huppert 2021
Images © Michèle Huppert and family 2021
Map © Judy Hollander 2021

The moral rights of the author have been asserted.

All rights reserved. No part of this publication may be reproduced, stored in a retrieval system or transmitted in any form by any means, electronic, mechanical, photocopying, recording or otherwise without the prior written permission of the author. Enquiries should be made to the publisher.

ISBN: 978-0-6488272-6-9

Edited by Georgie Raik-Allen
Editorial assistance by Romy Moshinsky
Designed by Marianna Berek-Lewis

CONTENTS

Foreword		xi
Chapter One	Childhood	15
Chapter Two	Paris	23
Chapter Three	Escape	45
Chapter Four	Malou	53
Chapter Five	Resistance	59
Chapter Six	Liberation	69
Chapter Seven	Peacetime	87
Postscript	Australia	103
Acknowledgements		120
Appendix A	Letters	126
Appendix B	Testimonies	136
Appendix C	IVRIA	144
Appendix D	OSE	150
References		152

With my beautiful mother, 1941

FOREWORD

This is the story of a remarkable woman whose exploits during World War II deserve to be known throughout the world.

Ruth preferred to leave the past behind. For her, the present was always far more important. She held no ambition to reveal details of our lives during the war years in a book. Instead, she kept her letters and documents neatly stored and her memories close to her heart.

It was not until my mother's death in 2007, when sorting through her belongings, that I found her precious papers. Recognising their great historical value, I decided to donate them to the Jewish Holocaust Centre in Melbourne where they would find international recognition and would be preserved, shared and celebrated. My memories were also awoken by the many photos, dates and inscriptions I was so fortunate to discover in my mother's files.

My painstaking research for this book was greatly aided by these documents, alongside the interviews and testimonies Ruth gave to the Jewish Holocaust Centre when she was in her late 80s, for which I am most grateful. I also drew heavily on online research, official war documents, historical events recounted in *Recollections of the Ivria* and two marvellous books that recount the role of brave French women like my mother during World War II: *Les Parisiennes* by Anne Sebba; and *Dans les pas des Resistants* by Danielle Darquié. Of course, I also relied on my own memories of the war years, when I was a young girl. Each source provided a missing piece in this giant jigsaw puzzle—the untold story of my mother's contribution to the liberation of France.

One of the questions often asked by readers of *Les Parisiennes*, is: was it justifiable for mothers working for the Resistance to compromise the safety of their children by using them as decoys in their missions?

As one of those children, my emphatic answer is yes.

This was a war with countless risks taken in the pursuit of freedom. I, daughter of Ruth, acknowledge with pride and honour, the small contribution I made in that fight for our freedom.

Me, 1943

Frederika and Ruth, c.1915

CHILDHOOD

Malou, my mother, was born with the name Ruth Altmann in Vienna on 6 October 1913 to Leo and Margaret Altmann (nee Berger). Leo was a widower with a daughter, Frederika, who was nine years old when he married Margaret. The family enjoyed a modest, middle-class lifestyle in a rented apartment. Leo was employed as a senior engineer in charge of the Austrian Railways from Vienna to Czechoslovakia, while Margaret ran the household.

During World War I, when Ruth was about three years old, the Altmann family moved to Teschen in eastern Czechoslovakia, near the small village where Leo was born and was registered in the army. Ruth recalled that the family was not exposed to many hardships during the war and that she would see her father whenever he was able to return from the front. In 1918, Leo was transferred to Krakow and the family moved to Poland.

Later that year, at the end of the war, they returned to Vienna and lived briefly with Ruth's maternal grandmother, Celestine Berger. Her parents and half-sister, Frederika, lived upstairs whilst Ruth was downstairs with her grandmother. It was difficult in the immediate post-war period to find accommodation but, with Leo's influence, the family eventually secured a small apartment to make their home. Sadly, at the end of 1918, Frederika died from the terrible influenza epidemic, the Spanish Flu, which was raging through Europe killing millions of people.[1] She was just 18 years old.

Leo and Margaret were not particularly religious, but lived a traditional Jewish life, observing the high holidays such as Pesach and Chanukah. Ruth described her family as 'modern Jews' who socialised with other Jewish families and got along well with their non-Jewish neighbours. They were dedicated Zionists inspired by the ideology of Theodor Herzl as well as the revisionist Zionist, Ze'ev Jabotinsky.[2] Leo was one of the founding members of the Vienna branch of the Zionist organisation IVRIA while Margaret was president of a Zionist women's group coincidentally also named Ruth. Leo attended the First Zionist Conference held in Basel, Switzerland in 1897 when he was 22 years old and became personally acquainted with Theodor Herzl and Chaim Weizmann, president of the Zionist Organization and, later, the first president of Israel. When Herzl died in 1904, Leo was one of many passionate Zionists to form a guard of honour at his funeral.

From a very young age, Ruth would accompany her parents to their Zionist meetings held in a three-room apartment at Tuerkenstrasse 9 in Vienna. Years later, a replica of the room was constructed in the Herzl Museum in Israel. When visiting that museum as an adult, Ruth was moved to see a reproduction of the large portrait of Herzl that had hung in the Vienna meeting room she had visited so often as a child.

---

1. The Spanish Flu infected 500 million people around the world. More than 50 million—possibly up to 100 million—people died (three to five percent of earth's population at the time), making it one of the deadliest epidemics in human history.

2. Jabotinsky cofounded the Jewish Legion of the British army in World War I. He also established several Jewish organisations in Palestine including Betar, Hatzohar, and the Irgun. He had a significant influence on Israeli politics through his involvement with the Herut party, which merged with other right wing parties to form the Likud Party in 1973.

CHILDHOOD

Ruth's half-sister, Frederika, c. 1908

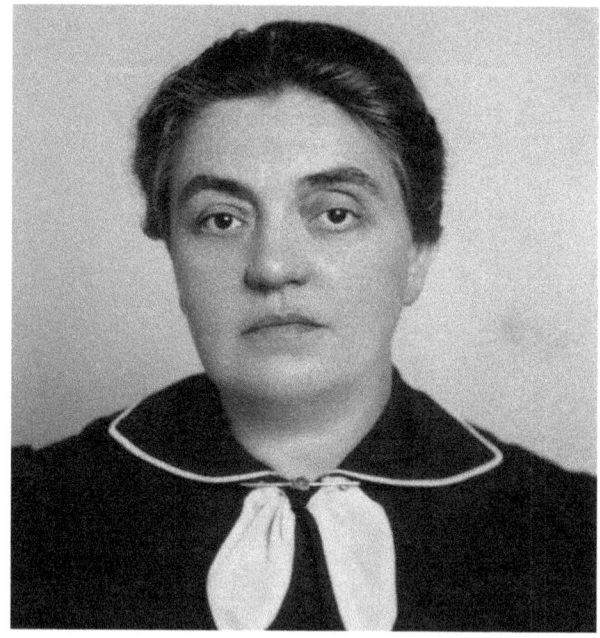

ABOVE: Ruth's father, Leo Altmann, 1938
BELOW: Ruth's mother, Margaret Altmann, 1938

Her parents' fervent Zionist idealism had a deep influence on Ruth's Jewish identity and the choices she made throughout her life. They would have been immensely proud of the life their daughter forged for herself.

Ruth grew into a beautiful young woman who participated in all the social and recreational activities of the time, including playing ice hockey and swimming for the Jewish sports club Hakoah. She attended a local primary school up to the sixth grade before enrolling into a Jewish girls' 'gymnasium', a high school where she obtained her matriculation.

One incident that occurred when Ruth was about 10 years old demonstrates her formidable character from an early age. A teacher at her primary school asked the students to remove all their jewellery. Ruth later recalled: "I was wearing a Magen David on a chain. A girl asked, 'Are you taking off your dog chain?' so I slapped her twice on her face. The next day my mother came with me to school where I explained to the headmistress and had to apologise in front all the other students. I said to the girl, 'I will forgive you, but I will never forget your insult'."

Ruth's passion, defiance and contempt for injustice would remain her defining characteristics throughout her long life.

Ruth, 1929

CHILDHOOD

Ruth with her parents, 1931

My parents, newly married, in Paris

PARIS

After completing her matriculation, in July 1931, Ruth moved to Paris where she studied French at Sorbonne University and learnt all facets of fashion design. During this period, to support herself, she found a job with a Jewish furrier.

In Paris, Ruth missed her parents but enjoyed the company of other Jewish friends, including my father, Fred Kneppel. Also from Vienna, Fred had moved to England after his matriculation to study English. He had then joined Ruth in Paris where he learnt the techniques required to operate large knitting machines.

In 1933, Ruth and Fred returned to Vienna to get married at their local synagogue in front of their families. The wedding was a modest affair and the couple enjoyed a brief honeymoon before returning to Paris where they lived in a one-bedroom apartment in the city's 11th arrondissement. As a wedding present, Leo and Margaret gave Ruth and Fred money to purchase a knitting machine that they could use to produce woollen garments, such as jumpers and vests. They established a knitting business in a single vacant room in an old building a few minutes from their apartment.

Fred, now an expert at operating the knitting machinery, created the fabric. Ruth made the patterns, cut the fabric and produced the finished garments.

LEFT: Fred's father, Smelko, 1906
RIGHT: Fred's mother, Frieda, 1913

PARIS

Fred with his mother, c. 1914

Fred (left) on holidays with his family, 1919

LEFT: Kneppel family, Fred, Smelko, Frieda & Curt, c. 1932
RIGHT: Curt & Ilse, in Vienna before the war

Their knitwear range was in huge demand and they worked very hard, often up to 18 hours a day, to fill their orders, many of which came from the prominent knitwear company, Tricosa.

In their limited spare time, Ruth and Fred enjoyed socialising with their Jewish friends and eating out at local restaurants. Life had not yet changed for the Jewish population of Paris, but my parents and their friends were becoming increasingly concerned by the reports of anti-Jewish incidents throughout Europe. As a politically engaged and well-informed Zionist with a sound Jewish education, Ruth was particularly attuned to these reports and was profoundly affected.

In Vienna, Ruth and Fred's families faced growing danger. On 12 March 1938, German troops marched into Austria and annexed the country into the 'Greater German Reich' on the pretext of protecting ethnic Germans and fulfilling Hitler's desire for territorial expansion. Policies of 'Aryanisation' were implemented in the immediate aftermath of the Anschluss and persecution of the local Jewish community intensified, resulting in the emigration of many Austrian Jews.[3]

While Leo and Margaret chose to remain in Vienna during this tumultuous time, Fred's parents, Smelko[4] and Frieda, sought refuge with Ruth and Fred in Paris. Fred's younger brother, Curt, and his fiancée, Ilse, fled to England where they married.[5]

---

3. By the end of 1941, 130,000 Jews had left Vienna. Most had to leave behind all of their property, but were forced to pay the Reich Flight Tax, a tax on all émigrés from Nazi Germany. The majority of the Jews who had stayed in Vienna were later murdered in the Holocaust.

4. Smelko Kneppel was born on 23 August 1883, one of 13 children. Of Smelko's 12 siblings, one died in childhood, one died before the war, four perished in the Holocaust, and the fate of the others remains unknown. He married Frieda Birken in Poland on 4 October 1909 and worked as a broker dealing with used metal.

5. After the birth of their son Tom in England, Curt and Ilse migrated and permanently settled in the USA. They later had a second son, Peter.

LEFT: Fred, 1929
RIGHT: Fred on holiday in Le Crotoy, 1932

When France and England declared war on Germany, after the invasion of Poland in September 1939, Ruth was six months pregnant with me. As foreigners and Jews, my parents and paternal grandparents were in grave danger and were advised to flee Paris. They closed their small factory and, together with their beloved dog Sultan, travelled north to settle in Le Crotoy[6], a small fishing village in the Somme estuary where they had previously spent their summer holidays. A lovely couple they had befriended during earlier trips, Mr and Mrs Potin, managed to find them safe refuge in a dilapidated farm on the outskirts of town.

In the middle of a freezing winter, with few provisions, and only cold water from a well outside, Ruth gave birth to a healthy baby girl on 21 December 1939. They named me Michèle. Ongoing anxiety about the war and grief following the death of Sultan caused my mother's breastmilk to dry up but, thankfully, the farmer allowed my parents to take milk directly from the cow in the field to feed me. Despite the deprivations, I flourished in those first few months of my life.

After the quiet first eight months of the war in France, known as the 'Phoney War', in the spring of 1940, German forces rapidly conquered the Netherlands, Luxembourg and Belgium and began their descent on France. Once again, my family was forced to flee, with many other refugees, along the heavily bombarded road towards Paris. It must have been a harrowing journey for my parents, travelling more than 200 kilometres with an infant and my grandparents.

---

6. During a visit to Le Crotoy in early 1992, I discovered that the town is a popular summer holiday fishing resort with an infamous past. Joan of Arc was imprisoned in the town by her people before being delivered by them to Rouen to be burnt. A beautiful, ultra-modern church has been erected at that site in her memory.

When they returned to Paris, Ruth and Fred found that their apartment and factory had been totally denuded of all contents, including the valuable knitting and sewing machines they had been forced to leave behind when they had fled.

Our family found small, temporary accommodation at 88 Rue des Boulets, in their familiar neighbourhood, the 11th arrondissement. However, without their knitting machines, my parents were unable to resume their garment-making business and were forced to take whatever jobs they could find to augment their depleted savings.

The German army marched into Paris on 14 June. Ruth later described the scene as she walked through a market: "One side of the street was filled with wagons overflowing with fruit and vegetables, and on the other side of the street I suddenly saw German soldiers approaching."

With the occupation of Paris, my parents' French naturalisation process was postponed and at the local police headquarters, they were required to register their names, address, religion and origin. From that point, Ruth and Fred, as Austrian Jews, were categorised as enemy aliens. This information was later used to prepare lists of foreigners and Jews for deportation.

A week after marching on Paris, on 22 June 1940, France and Germany signed an armistice, dividing the country along a boundary known as the demarcation line into two zones: a German-occupied zone in northern and western France, and the free zone in the south, administered under the leadership of World War I hero Marshal Philippe Pétain, with headquarters in Vichy. On 10 July, the French National Assembly voted to give plenary power to the Vichy government and Pétain assumed authoritarian powers. A separate agreement allowed Italy to take control of a small occupation zone in the southeast. Refusing to accept the armistice, General Charles de Gaulle fled to England

PARIS

My parents' formal wedding photo, 1933

My parents, 1935

My mother and Sultan before the war

where he established a government-in-exile, known as the Free French Forces (FFF), and directed the Resistance.

With the Germans occupying Paris, the persecution of Jews began in earnest and our lives were increasingly under threat. In 1941, all Jewish businesses were forced to close, including Tricosa, the knitwear company where Ruth and Fred had found work. And, from May 1942, we were obliged to wear the yellow Star of David on our clothes. My parents became ever more fearful as they began to hear rumors that the French police, under orders of the Nazis, were arresting Jews for deportation.

Anne Sebba documents the arrests in her book *Les Parisiennes*: "The first wave of arrests took place on the 14 May 1941 when 3710 foreigner Jews were arrested, followed three months later after a raid on the 11th arrondissement by a further 4230 Jews, both French and foreigners; in December, 734 prominent French Jews and 250 immigrants Jews were seized."[7]

Our family moved constantly in an attempt to evade the police. Thanks to my mother's fearless nature and defiant attitude, I had no sense of danger and our manoeuvres seemed to me like an elaborate game of hide-and-seek.

Throughout this difficult time, Ruth managed to continue sending parcels to her parents in Vienna and to correspond through postcards. In their letters, my grandparents wrote veiled descriptions of their lives, including information about their friends and family members in Vienna, while at the same time cautioning Ruth to be careful when writing. In one letter they wrote: "If you do not receive a letter from us for a few weeks, do not despair as it is possible that we too will soon be resettled like so many other acquaintances... we are calm and completely devoted to God, we do not despair, even if we have to leave."

---

7. Anne Sebba, *Les Parisiennes*, St Martin's Press, 2016, p.89

ABOVE: One of the letters my grandparents wrote to us from Vienna
BELOW: My grandparents sent me this letter for my second birthday

MALOU

Me at 11 months, November 1940

My grandparents' letters provide bittersweet insight into their special character. I particularly treasure two tender letters addressed to me on the occasions of my first and second birthdays. In November 1941 they wrote: "You are quickly approaching your second birthday and your grandparents who live far away would like to congratulate you… you have become a little lady, who is smiling cheekily from the photograph on our wall, filling us with hope of a happy reunion."

Soon after the arrival of my second birthday card, letters from my maternal grandparents abruptly ceased. Due to their Zionist affiliation, Margaret and Leo were rounded up and deported on one of the first transports of Austrian Jews to the East. On 11 January 1942, they were forced onto a train departing for Riga in Latvia.[8] However, the Jews on the transport never arrived at the intended destination as they were all removed from the train and shot in the open. Hitler was furious that the mass murder had occurred in front of many officers and other witnesses and ordered that all future convoys proceed directly to their destination where extermination could be implemented out of sight.

Meanwhile in Paris, my paternal grandfather, Smelko, who had evaded the police twice, was finally captured and taken first to Chateauroux, then to Gurs, a concentration camp in southwest France. By that time, my grandmother Frieda had also been arrested and both were taken to the train station for deportation to Drancy, the internment camp in Paris. At the station, patrolled by German and Italian soldiers, Fred managed to bribe an Italian guard to let his sick mother out but could not do the same for Smelko. His failed attempt to save his father was

---

8. We did not receive official confirmation of the fate of my grandparents until 1946.

a heavy burden that my father carried for the rest of his life. On 6 March 1943, Smelko departed France on convoy No. 51 for its final destinations, the extermination camps of Maidanek and Sorbibor.[9]

***

In Paris, Ruth and Fred had become great friends with the owner of a local bistro, 'La Tante'[10], as she was known to us, and she would always alert them to imminent raids by the French police. One day when Ruth arrived at the bistro to visit her friend, she was met with a pointed look towards two men in civilian clothing who were making enquiries about our family.[11]

Ruth left the bistro immediately and did not return. It was now imperative that our family escape from Paris.

---

9. Source: Memorial of the Shoah France, deportation document.
10. 'The aunt'.
11. Ruth recounted this story in her testimony for the Jewish Holocaust Centre in Melbourne.

Paris, near my parent's factory and La Tante's bistro
From left: La Tante, unknown friend, Fred, Ruth & Margret, with Sultan

My parents in Paris, December 1937

With my mother, 1940

I had no idea of the danger we were in after escaping Paris for the Biederbeck's home in the countryside, 1942

ESCAPE

Somehow, with the assistance of friends, we managed to acquire false Algerian identity papers. Ruth and Fred spoke with an accent similar to Algerian French and my mother's colouring was dark enough that we passed for Algerian Christians.

We removed the yellow stars from our clothing and, together with my paternal grandmother, whom I called Omi, we left Paris to seek refuge with my father's cousin, Ilse, in the countryside. Ilse was married to a non-Jewish man, Hans Biederbeck, so we felt somewhat safer in their home. The Biederbeck family lived in a lovely house with a garden full of fruit trees and I enjoyed playing with their son and daughter, Christiane, who was the same age as me. It was a wonderful diversion from the mood of fear and foreboding in Paris. However, my parents knew that we were in danger while we remained in the occupied zone and, after a week or two, we reluctantly farewelled the family. By the time the police came to the house looking for us, we had already left.[12]

La Tante, the bistro owner, had a niece who had frequently come to Paris to visit before the war and had also become good friends with my mother. She lived in the Lot-et-Garonne in the

---

12. The Beiderbeck family survived the war and, on one of our visits back to France, they spoke about possibly moving to Australia. However, we lost contact in the following decades and never found out whether they emigrated.

free zone of southern France and offered to assist our family to find refuge in the area. So, on the move again!

My parents, grandmother and I made our way by train to the border separating the occupied north and the free France of the south. After disembarking, we found the border crowded with people like us, desperately attempting to escape. In 1942, I was not yet three years old so, to quicken their pace, my parents carried me in a large shopping bag. German soldiers and other officials in civilian clothes were heavily patrolling the border to unoccupied France. They could have randomly stopped us, interrogated my parents and demanded to see our papers. We were so very lucky that no one approached us.

Once safely across the border, my father thought we would draw less attention if we travelled in two smaller groups. My father and grandmother went to join friends who had escaped Paris and were living in Nice and Monte Carlo, on the southeast coast of France. The region was occupied by the Italians and it was considered less dangerous for Jews at the time. My mother and I, now alone, took the overcrowded train, standing room only, into the free zone of Dordogne. This separation was a turning point in the private lives of my parents.

We arrived in the town of Fumel where we sought refuge with an acquaintance of La Tante. Even in the unoccupied zone Ruth remained vigilant and we never remained in one place for too long. A few days later we moved to Villeneuve-sur-Lot to stay with the niece of La Tante, before moving once again to a room in the home of an elderly couple. In all the humble homes we sought refuge, our hosts were very kind and asked no questions.

After a few weeks, we were given the address of a nearby farm where an illegal refugee from Italy, Mario, lived with his elderly mother, known to all as Nonna. Mario had fled Mussolini's fascism after losing a leg fighting in the war.

Making friends with my cousin, Christiane Biederbeck

My mother and me at the farm, 1943

As young as I was, at just three years old, I vividly recall our journey to the farm along a pitch-dark, wooded, country road on a borrowed bicycle. I sat behind my mother, clinging to her waist as she cautioned me to be absolutely silent and pedaled towards our destination. What an experience for a young mother with a three-year-old child! This gutsiness surfaced many times throughout her life.

As fellow refugees, Mario and Nonna greeted us warmly to the farm. The old farm house comprised one large room with a big open fireplace used for cooking and heating, and two other rooms for sleeping. A rudimentary toilet and washing facilities were found outside. Ruth and I were given the small back room with one very high, old single bed. Worried that I might fall, Ruth placed the mattress on the floor for me and she slept on the hard, wooden base. At all times, my safety and wellbeing remained my mother's highest priority.

Over the next few months, despite the hardships and dangers, I spent many precious hours with Nonna at the farm. Together, we collected the few brussels sprouts and potatoes we could find in the fields, and spent hours playing with her little dog and pet rabbit. I will always treasure the memory of the chocolate pudding Nonna miraculously made for me, which appeared at the front door of the farm one Easter morning. I still wonder how she managed to make the delicious treat with the shortages we experienced, to bring such joy to a little girl in an ugly world. It was many years later that I was able to appreciate how different and tragic the war experiences of other children had been.

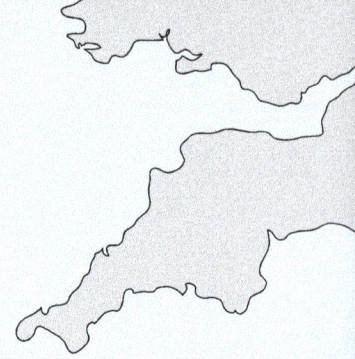

MALOU

FRANCE
1940–1944

═══ Ruth's Journey

⋯⋯ Fred & Omi's Journey

↓ Normandy Invasion, 6 June 1944

☐ German Occupation Zone, 1940

▨ Area intended for German Settlement

▨ Third Reich Annexations of 1940

☐ Free Zone until 11 Nov 1942

▨ Italian Occupation Zone, Nov 1942–Sept 1943

▨ Italian Occupation Zone, 1940

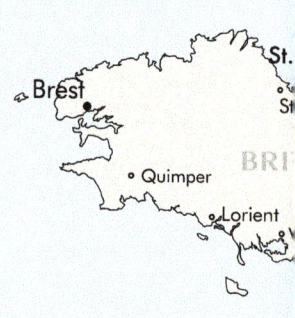

ATLANTIC OCEAN

BAY OF BISCAY

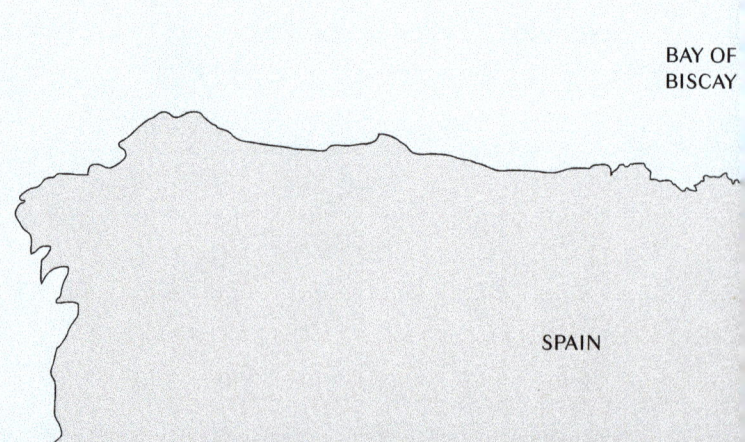

SPAIN

With Mario at the farm

MALOU

While living with Mario and Nonna, Ruth was introduced to other illegal refugees, mostly Italian, who lived on nearby farmland. They were very kind to us. Knowing that we were short of food, they often shared their own meagre supplies with us. They understood the unspoken rules of wartime and never asked us questions about our background nor the circumstances that led us to seek refuge so far from home. Although there were no other children around, it felt to me like I was suddenly part of a large, warm family.

My mother soon learnt that Mario and the other refugees were underground guerilla fighters known as Maquisards, some of the thousands of rural combatants operating in small independent cells to resist Nazi war efforts and harass the collaborators. The guerilla fighters comprised of men and some women, who had fled to the mountains and forests to avoid conscription into Vichy's *Service du Travail Obligatoire*[13] which provided forced labour for Germany, as well as illegal refugees such as left-wing veterans of the Spanish Civil War, communists, and Jews fleeing persecution in Eastern Europe.

---

13. The Service du Travail Obligatoire (Compulsory Work Service) led to the forced enlistment and deportation of more than 600,000 French workers to Nazi Germany to provide forced labour for the German war effort between June 1942 and July 1944.

In November 1942, the German army invaded France's free zone and a few months later, on 1 March 1943, the demarcation line was officially annulled. From that time, Germany occupied all of France. To avoid capture and deportation to Germany, and to assist in the fight to liberate their adopted homeland, guerilla fighters became increasingly organised into active Resistance groups known as Maquis.[14]

Motivated by a fierce hatred of the Germans and determined to avenge her parents' deportation, my brave mother, just 30 years old, joined the local Maquis group, Prosper. Recruited as an *'agent de liaison'*, she was provided with a new false identity as a Christian Algerian woman, and was given the *nom de guerre*, Malou[15], along with the military identification number, 60.

Anonymity was considered most important and missions were only ever known by the agent and their Resistance chief. Like many Maquis groups, Prosper operated in wooded areas where Maquisards could easily hide and it was possible to conceal whatever small arms they possessed. Funding from Resistance headquarters was negligible, and Maquisards had to be resourceful and protect their weapons for use in future missions. From the time the demarcation line was annulled, Malou's assignments became increasingly perilous.

The Maquis were so successful in disrupting German military plans and harassing the local collaborating authorities that, in early 1943, the Vichy government established a brutal paramilitary force called the Milice to combat Resistance activity. The Milice assisted the Germans in rounding up Jews and Resistance fighters

---

14. The term 'Maquis' came from the name of the scrub that covered much of the high ground in southern France where many guerilla Resistance groups hid.

15. I could not find any official documentation revealing her new surname, but even as a young child, I do recall vividly that my name during this time was Michèle Cinousi.

for deportation, used torture to extract information, and executed its prisoners. The Milice was considered even more dangerous in the region than the Gestapo and SS because it was comprised of native Frenchmen who understood local dialects and had extensive knowledge of the local countryside and people.

In Villeneuve-sur-Lot, Malou became aware of a man called Tony who seemed to be observing her movements wherever she went. Unbeknown to her, Tony belonged to a local Resistance group and was charged with checking on new recruits to ensure that they were not undercover enemy agents. He was suspicious of Malou. With her language skills, self-assured attitude and good grooming, she did not resemble the typical refugee Maquisard woman. One day he noticed her signet ring and asked about the discrepancy between the initials 'RK' (Ruth Kneppel) and her name, Malou. She had no choice but to divulge the truth of her identity to reassure him that she was not a fascist sympathiser attempting to infiltrate the Resistance. This incident demonstrated the desperately high stakes and the vigilance of the Resistance in protecting the safety of its agents and the secrecy of its missions.

Meanwhile, my father Fred and grandmother remained in Nice where Italians sympathetic to the plight of Jews helped to secure them new passports. At some point during 1943, my father came to the farm and took me to stay with him and my grandmother. I remember this as a very happy time for me. However, after some months, Fred was arrested by the police and was imprisoned in Lyon. Upon hearing the news, Malou travelled to Nice to join us.

I remained with my grandmother whilst Malou went to the police station in an effort to secure Fred's release. Unfortunately, she too was arrested and interrogated for six hours by the chief of the police. During the interrogation, she proudly admitted to being Jewish and having a young child waiting for her. She told him that if she was deported, she would try to escape to be with her daughter. By an incredible stroke of luck, and unbeknown to her, the chief was also an undercover Resistance fighter. He let Malou and Fred go free, under the protection of the two police officers who had originally arrested her.

After this dangerous incident, my father returned to my grandmother in Nice while my mother and I travelled back to the farm on the outskirts of Villeneuve, where Malou continued her work for the Resistance.

LEFT: With my father in Nice before his arrest, 1943
RIGHT: Summer, 1943

Malou's *Forces Françaises de l'Interieur (FFI)* badge

RESISTANCE

Between 1943 and August 1944, Malou undertook numerous dangerous missions with gutsy determination. These missions involved reconnaissance work, delivering hidden weapons for clandestine operations, relaying messages between Maquis groups, and reporting on German conversations overheard on trains, in bistros and on the streets. When not on a train, much of her work was conducted on bicycle which allowed her to move around without attracting undue suspicion and to access locations not possible in a car.

One of her regular duties was to memorise information about the enemy that would assist the Resistance in their efforts to sabotage German convoys or disrupt collaboration of the Vichy officials. After receiving a verbal message from an operative, she would cycle into the nearby chestnut forest to pass on the critical information.

One such mission assisted Maquisards who were hiding in the forest and desperately in need of food. She cycled to the town hall, noted its layout and surroundings, and relying on her photographic memory, drew a plan of that building. Later that night, the fighters used her plan to raid the town hall and steal ration tickets.

Malou (back, right) with her Maquis Resistance batallion, Prosper

Another important operation was to deliver a revolver, hidden in the depth of her bag, to a bistro where it would later be used to shoot a senior SS officer as he was driven past the bistro. Such was the shortage of weapons available to the Maquis, that Malou later returned to the bistro to retrieve the revolver and return it to its hiding spot.

Women were in high demand in the Resistance, as they were less conspicuous than men[16] and less likely to be stopped or questioned when passing through German checkpoints on foot or bicycle. Women rarely engaged in military operations but their role as couriers of messages, and even weapons concealed in prams and shopping baskets, was highly valued. Female participation in the Resistance became a most valuable asset in the fight for freedom.

Malou was the ideal operative to carry out Resistance activities. With her false Algerian passport, language skills and indomitable attitude, she could travel widely and conduct her missions without attracting suspicion. Malou was always well dressed to give the impression of a woman from the city rather than a refugee hiding under false papers on a farm. Fortunately, La Tante had provided my mother with some nice clothes. However, even in the most humble attire, my mother and I were always well groomed and looked smart.

Malou had tremendous composure, especially in dire situations, and showed stoicism in adversity. At times, she was asked to show her papers or open her bag, which fortunately was never thoroughly searched. On one such occasion, a German soldier looked through her bag and failed to discover the revolver

---

16. That same lack of visibility meant the role of women in the Resistance was overlooked for many years after the war. Women represented 15 to 20 percent of French Resistance fighters and 15 percent of political deportations from France to Nazi concentration camps. However, of 1,036 members of the Resistance honoured by Charles de Gaulle in the Order of Liberation, only six were female.

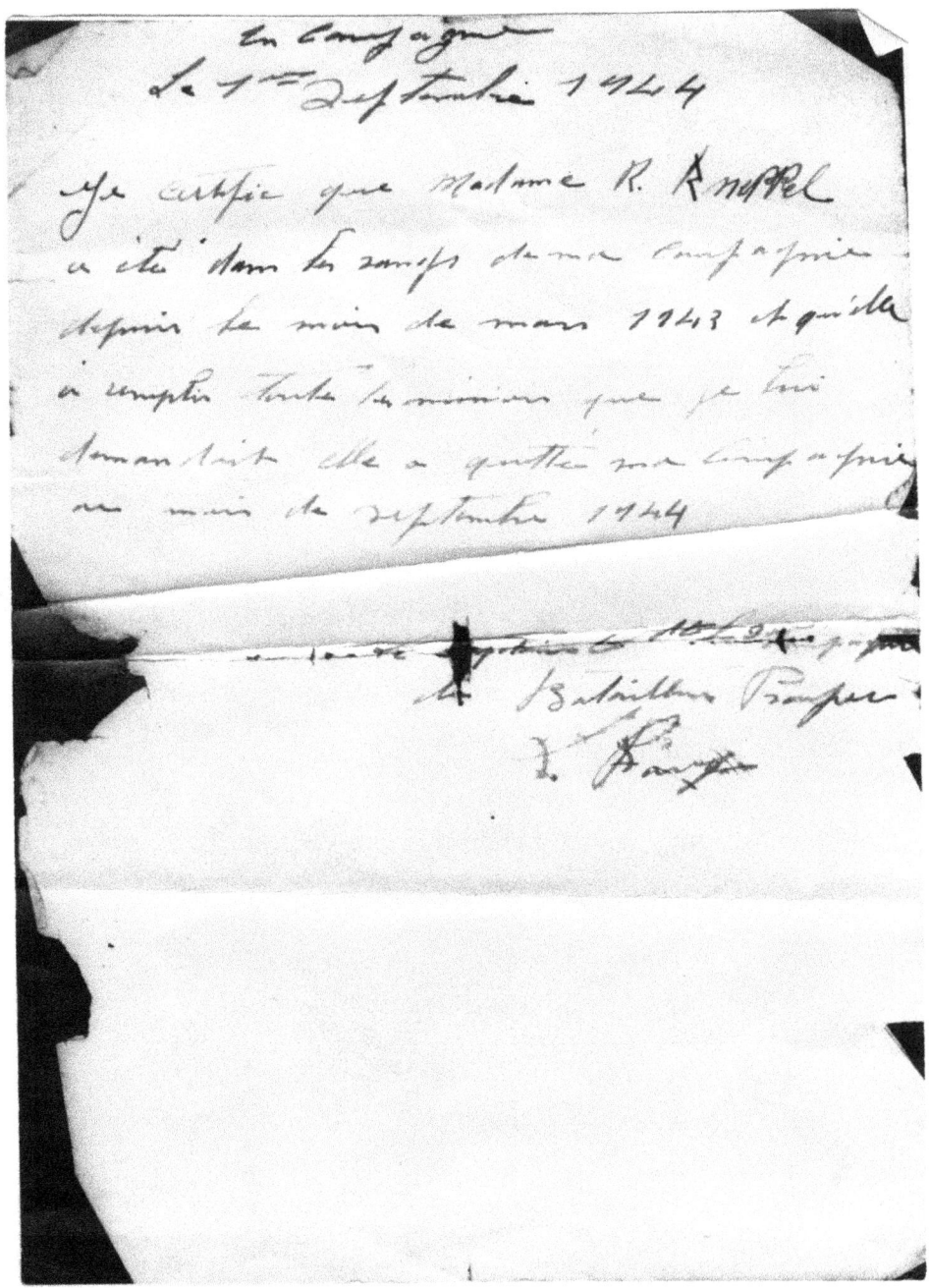

Testimony regarding Malou's Resistance work, written in the battlefield by the captain of the Prosper battalion

I often accompanied my mother on her missions. With her immaculate grooming and in the company of an innocent child she never raised any suspicions.

hidden in its depth. Despite the grave danger, Malou's composure would never falter, and she always spoke to the authorities with polite conviction, which no doubt ensured our survival.

I often accompanied my mother in train carriages full of SS officers while she listened in on their conversations in German. In many ways, I was the perfect ruse for Malou. Few would suspect that a confident, well-presented mother travelling with a young child was undertaking a dangerous secret mission.

From a very young age, I was taught good behaviour, correct table manners, and to remain quiet when required. I learnt to recognize unspoken messages from my mother: slight movements of her head transmitted negative or positive messages, and the lowering of her eyes told me when I need to be silent.

During those terrible war years, I was a mere toddler with virtually no other children for playmates. However, I was always well cared for with love from doting adults. I still had my mother and always felt secure. We were never apart for too long and I learnt from her to accept these perilous times as part of our life.

In February 1944, the stage was set for a massive jailbreak at the Eysses prison in Villeneuve-sur-Lot, where the Vichy government had detained 1200 political prisoners, including many leaders of the Resistance. Malou's Prosper group, along with other Maquis cells active in the region, were mobilised to assist in the operation. Maquisards prepared detainees for insurrection, smuggling into the prison small arms, newspapers, even a radio, with the assistance of sympathetic guards. Malou never revealed her specific involvement in the mission, but she would have likely played a vital role supplying arms and relaying messages between prisoners and local Maquis groups.

However, on 19 February, the political prisoners became impatient with last minute delays and launched an uprising before final preparations were in place. Malou later reported that she, along with other Maquisards who were waiting on the outside to assist the prisoners, heard gunshots from within. After waiting for many hours, they realised that no one had escaped. A large number of prisoners were shot, and many were transported to Dachau concentration camp where they continued to fight for their survival. Only a few returned after the war.

Malou's commander, captain Ferdinand Gaumy, later wrote an official report detailing her Resistance work during this time. "I certify with honour to have employed Madame Ruth Kneppel (*nom de guerre* Malou) as a liaison agent from January 1943 till February 1944. She was continuously in contact with political detainees, ensuring they were supplied with arms and food, and always discharged her work with *sang-froid* and courage. With perfect knowledge of the German language, we were able to obtain information on the enemy on the way to our town, information always exact and often of the greatest importance. She exemplified, whatever the circumstance, audacity and *sang-froid* worthy of all commendation."

* * *

A refugee couple from Alsace-Lorraine (a German-speaking region of France) who lived on another part of the farm, owned a clandestine radio. Malou and other Maquisards would often gather at their home in the evenings to listen to German radio transmissions regarding the progress of the war. Not knowing that Malou understood German perfectly, the couple would translate information for her to pass onto her Resistance chief. This information included details about German army activities, such as the movements of troops and battalions, that could be used to disrupt the enemy's plans.

One evening in early June, on one of her regular visits to listen to the secret radio, Malou heard coded messages, transmitted by the BBC from London, signalling to Resistance groups that a significant Allied invasion was imminent and sabotage operations should begin.

The following day, Tuesday 6 June 1944, the Allies landed on the beaches of Normandy in the largest seaborne invasion in history. The operation, often referred to as 'D-Day', began the liberation of German-occupied France and is considered a turning point in World War II.

Thousands of Resistance fighters, including Maquisards, were mobilised to engage in Resistance activities timed to co-ordinate with the Allied invasion, including sabotaging the rail system, destroying electrical facilities, cutting telephone cables, and disrupting enemy convoys, to slow down German reinforcements. The Maquisards of the Lot-et-Garonne played an active role in these operations.[17]

Once the Allies had secured a foothold in France, the government of Free France attempted to incorporate the many independent Maquis cells into De Gaulle's Resistance movement, which had been renamed *Forces Francaises de l'Interieur (FFI)*. Malou continued her Resistance work as a member of the FFI and was allocated the number 184619, which was inscribed on her badge. FFI units were established throughout the country, including a committee in Villeneuve-sur-Lot, headed by Malou. From that time, Maquisards worked as part of a united and coordinated effort in the fight against the German forces.

---

17. The Maquis were recognised at the end of the war by DeGaulle, and named 'armee secrete'.

Reunited with Omi after liberation

LIBERATION

Operation Dragoon, the landing of Allied forces in Provence on 15 August 1944, spearheaded the liberation of southern France.

In the early morning of 19 August, convoys of enemy soldiers evacuated the nearby town of Agen, signalling the imminent liberation of the surrounding area. In Villeneuve, Prosper was commanded to display its flag. Six days later, on 25 August, the Germans in Paris surrendered to the Allies and the French government[18], ending four years of occupation. The remnants of the German army began a hasty retreat eastward.

Having returned from London, Charles de Gaulle, leader of the Free French Government and head of the French Resistance, led a victory parade along the Champs Élysées and entered the Place de la Concorde. De Gaulle had underestimated the role of the Maquisards, later referred to as the 'secret army'[19], in the liberation of France, but later acknowledged the significant role that the 25,000 guerilla fighters had played, and declared that

---

18. General Dietrich von Choltitz, commander of the German garrison, defied an order by Adolf Hitler to blow up Paris' landmarks and burn the city to the ground in the days before its liberation.

19. The secret army in the Lot-et-Garonne included Malou's group, Prosper.

their clandestine, patriotic and courageous activities demonstrated values that were characteristically French.

After the liberation of Paris, Resistance work ceased and Maquisards had the choice of joining regular armed groups to continue fighting the Germans in the north, or returning home. The vast majority immediately returned to civilian life.[20] Around this time, Prosper disbanded and my mother shed her *nom de guerre*, Malou, to became known, once again, as Ruth.

On 24 December 1944, Ruth received an official 'ordre de mission' from her FFI commander to travel to Nice for top secret 'propaganda' business. Ruth never divulged the nature of this secret mission. It was a wonderful opportunity for us to both travel to Nice and reunite with my beloved father and grandmother. Though only five years old, I vividly recall that we hitched a ride in an American military convoy, which was the only official mode of transport while the war continued to rage through much of Europe. During the trip, I sat in the front seat with my mother eating chocolate and trying to work out what to do with the strange chewing gum an American soldier had offered me. I also remember, while walking in Nice, seeing my first ever African American soldier and telling my mother, in a voice loud enough make him smile, "*chololat ce monsieur*—this man is like chocolate".

After the liberation of France, the country was swept with a wave of executions of collaborators, including an estimated 25,000 to 35,000 Milicien. Others were tried and imprisoned while some managed to escape and flee to Germany.

---

20. It is such a shame that so few Maquisards left testimony regarding their attempts to sabotage the German occupation of France. In their haste to return to normal, civilian life, only about one fifth handed over their documents or were debriefed, which would have provided invaluable records for historians of the Resistance. Thus the importance of Malou's story.

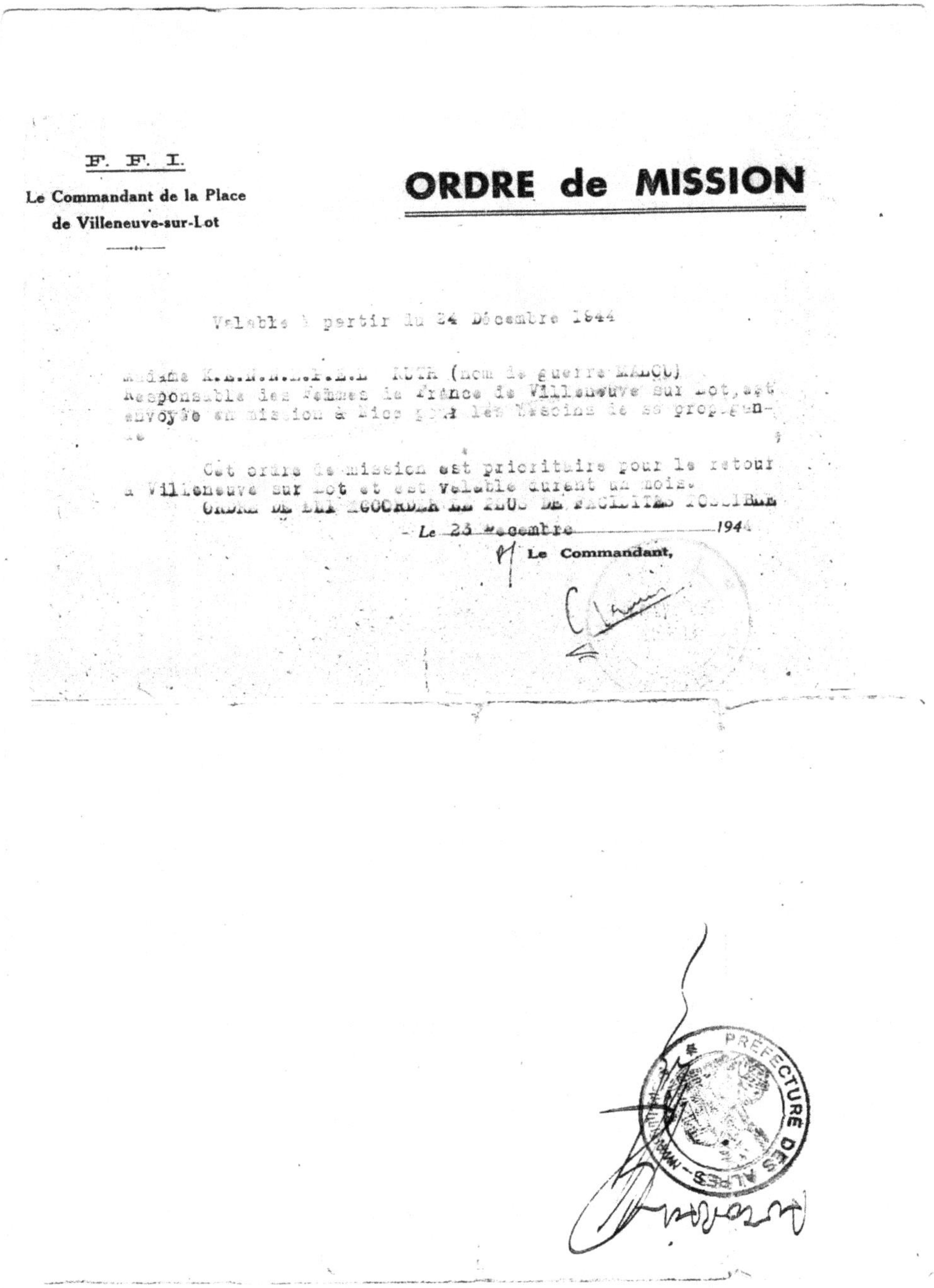

F. F. I.

Le Commandant de la Place
de Villeneuve-sur-Lot

ORDRE de MISSION

Valable à partir du 24 Décembre 1944

Madame [illegible] RUTH (nom de guerre MALOU)
Responsable des Femmes de France de Villeneuve sur Lot, est envoyée en mission à Nice pour les besoins de sa propagande

Cet ordre de mission est prioritaire pour le retour à Villeneuve sur Lot et est valable durant un mois.
ORDRE DE LUI ACCORDER LE PLUS DE FACILITES POSSIBLE

Le 23 Décembre 1944

Le Commandant,

An order from the FFI to travel to Nice on a secret mission

My family reunited after liberation

My mother shed her *nom de guerre* Malou and became known as Ruth once again

Villeneuve UFF, 1944

With two of Ruth's colleagues from the Villeneuve UFF, 1945

MALOU

CENTRE

NOM Kneppel née le 6 oct. 1913 né allemann
Prénoms Ruth
Adresse 2 Passage Cantoro
Date et lieu de naissance 6. oct. 1913 à Vienne
Nationalité ex- Autrichienne

Service militaire { 1) Classe
{ 2) État de Service

Date de naturalisation s'il y a lieu

Pour les étrangers { N° carte identité N° 40 CMS 5066
{ Validité 31-12-45
{ Travailleur ou non

Avez-vous fait partie d'un mouvement de résistance? oui lequel? Bataillon "Prosper"
Situation de famille mariée
Enfants (dates de naissance) où sont-ils? que font-ils
21 déc. 1939 avec moi école maternelle

Le conjoint travaille-t-il non
Charges de famille 1 enfant et belle-mère (dont le mari déporté)
Date d'entrée 1 juin 1945
Engagé par qui Mme Salomon
Appointements
Etes-vous inscrit aux Assurances Sociales? oui
A quelle caisse N° d'immatriculation 13 4702789 10
                                            BORDEAUX
Etes-vous inscrit aux Allocations Familiales?
A quelle caisse? N° d'immatriculation
Fonction actuelle assistante
Fonctions successives s'il y a lieu
Formation et diplômes baccalauréat
Langues étrangères connues allemand
Emplois exercés antérieurement à l'entrée à l'O.S.E. responsable de l'U.F.F.
de Villeneuve (Lot et Gar.)
Projets ou désirs

16.6.45   Vu : Le chef du Centre,   Signature,
                                                     Kneppel Ruth

P. S. - Prière de demander à chacun, de nous adresser son curriculum vitæ manuscrit, et 2 photos de face de préférence.

Ruth's OSE application, June 1945

Throughout the country, between 10,000 to 30,000 women were accused of collaboration, and those suspected of having romantic liaisons with Germans were publicly humiliated by having their heads shaved. These women became known as 'the shorn' and were paraded through the streets on the back of open trucks. I can still recall seeing trucks carrying the shaved women, branded as traitors, as they were driven through Villeneuve.

General Pétain, the former head of Vichy France, would later be charged with treason. In August 1945 he was convicted and sentenced to death by firing squad, but de Gaulle commuted the sentence to life imprisonment before his execution. He died at home in 1951, aged 95.

In the Villeneuve-sur-Lot prison, political prisoners were freed and replaced by Nazi collaborators. Ruth sat on a panel of judges in the trial of these cases, a critical and gruesome task. She was also deeply involved in the significant work to transition France from war to peacetime and took on a number of roles to assist in these efforts. From June 1944 to April 1945 she represented the newly formed committee, the Comite Departemental de Liberation (CDL) and she also reported to Republican Garde Civic (GDC).

From 1943 to 1945, Ruth headed up the committee of Union des Femmes Francaises (UFF) in Villeneuve, one of the strongest and most active UFF groups in the region. As part of her role, she helped survivors secure food, shelter, clothing and assisted them in the search for surviving family members.

It was not until April 1945, when she had completed all the work assigned to her position at the UFF in Villeneuve, that Ruth left and applied for a position, offered by the American Joint[21], at the L'Oeuvre de Secours des Enfants (OSE), a Jewish

---

21. The American Jewish Joint Distribution Committee, also known as the Joint or the JDC, is a Jewish relief organisation that supports Jewish communities around the world through a range of social and community assistance programs.

AMERICAN JOINT DISTRIBUTION COMMITTEE
AUSTRIA SEARCH BUREAU
HQ USFA ARTISANS BUILDING APO 777 POSTMASTER NEW YORK CITY

Re: File:27535 Vienna, May 21st, 46
Paris Memo 465

Mr. Herrn Ruth Kneppel
Mrs. Frau Paris 11é 2 Passage Courtois
Miss Frl.

Dear friend:—
Lieber Freund!

The following is a report on your recent request for information about

Nachstehend geben wir Dir einen Bericht auf Deine Anfrage über

    Altmann Leo   1875
    2   Margarete 1887

    last addr. 9.Grundlg.1/7

Information secured:

Have been evacuated to Riga on Jan 11th, 42 and have not returned.

Not found: We regret that a search of our files has shown no person of that identity.

Wir bedauern, Dir mitteilen zu müssen, daß die angefragte(n) Person(en) in unserer Suchkartei nicht aufscheinen.

In process: Our search will be completed in _____ days, and you will hear
In Behandlung: from us further.

Ihre Anfrage wird voraussichtlich in _____ Tagen erledigt werden. Wir behalten uns vor, hierauf zurückzukommen.

Sincerely

Dr. J. Benson Saks
Chief Austrian Operations
AJDC

It wasn't until 1946 that my mother received confirmation from the Joint of her parents' fate

organisation dedicated to the rescue and assistance of refugee Jewish children.

In a letter to support her application, UFF delegate Simone Papon wrote: "Ruth Kneppel worked for the Resistance, transporting arms under the nose of the Germans…. she has done everything possible in her power to hasten the liberation of France, thus repaying back the debt of recognition to the nation who welcomed her."

Ruth began her work with the OSE on 8 May 1945, at the conclusion of the war in Europe and at a time when Dachau and surrounding German concentration camps were being liberated by the American army. Supporting refugee children as they were liberated from camps across Europe was the greatest task ever undertaken by the OSE.

On 10 June 1946, Ruth received a request, along with a military permit endorsed jointly by the Joint and the OSE, to accompany Rosa Roth, a 76-year-old Austrian woman whom she knew personally, to Vienna, the city of her childhood. She also received an official certificate of work, which was mandatory for travel in Europe at the time. The whole continent was in disarray with thousands of refugees languishing in displaced persons' camps, Nazis attempting to escape authorities, and governments working to restore order. Transport was strictly restricted, and no-one was permitted to travel alone or without a pass.

In Vienna, Ruth and Rosa stayed in an apartment provided by the Joint and, due to the scarcity of food, they were given the same ration boxes as soldiers. During that time, Ruth refused to speak German except on one occasion in a shop. Other customers had noted her US army insignia, and assuming she would not be able to understand, began talking derogatively about her. When walking out of the shop, Ruth turned around and in impeccable German told them exactly what she thought of them.

It was while she was in Vienna, that my mother received documentation from the authorities confirming that her parents "were evacuated to Riga on Jan 11th, '42 and have not returned". No other details were known about their fate. This news confirmed Ruth's worst fear that she would never see her parents again.

As part of her mission, Ruth was asked to visit a large hospital and to prepare a report on the conditions and availability of medical equipment. The hospital was full of people from displaced persons' camps, but it was very short on supplies. There were no syringes, no medication and the doctors and nurses struggled to provide basic health care.

The devastation she found in the decimated city of Vienna distressed my mother greatly and she cried every day. On her journey home to France, she became particularly upset as she travelled through Switzerland, which had remained neutral during the war, and noted that the country had escaped much of the despair and ruin that had ravaged most of Europe.[22]

---

22. Ruth was very emotional during this period in her life and found it difficult to describe in testimony provided many years later.

A memorial in Villeneuve lists the names of all the children in the town who died during the war

My father at a house in Villeneuve, 1945

LIBERATION

Me, Villeneuve, 1945

With my mother, April 1946

At the farm with Nonna after the war

Paris, 1952

PEACETIME

Having completed her mission in Vienna, Ruth finally returned to Paris, moving back into our apartment in Passage Courtois on the third floor. She found that once again, all the contents of the apartment, as well as the one-room factory located a couple of small lanes away, had been stolen during the German occupation. At the town hall, authorities were distributing supplies to returning residents and Ruth was able to acquire two beds, a table and two chairs. I arrived in Paris soon after, accompanied by friends of my parents who were returning from Nice. When my father and Omi followed, a few weeks later, we acquired more furniture.

Finally, after four years apart, my family was reunited in Paris and we began to piece our lives back together. The apartment included two spacious bedrooms, one for my parents and the other for my grandmother and me, as well as a small kitchen where we cooked and ate our meals, and a toilet with a private area for washing.

In October 1946, I was nearly seven years of age and finally able to start my formal schooling at the kindergarten attached to the local primary school for girls at Rue de la Roquette. Every day I walked to and from school with Denise, the 11-year-old daughter of another Jewish family who lived on the same floor as us and who had also recently returned to Paris. By the end of my first year, I had moved up to the first year of school, where I progressed rapidly, to complete primary school in 1950 at the age of 10.

For some time, Ruth worked for the OSE in three districts, helping many children reunite with surviving family members, as well as assisting with adoptions or other arrangements to secure homes for them. In August 1946, she completed her work with the OSE and returned to her prewar occupation in the knitwear fashion industry. Ruth designed and manufactured garments, working with a sewing machine and basic equipment in my parents' small factory while Fred found employment at Tricosa, whose owners had survived the war and reopened their business.

Eighteen months after our return to Paris, and many years since they had initiated the process before the war, my parents were finally naturalised as French citizens.

In 1947, my grandmother moved to New York to reunite with her other son, Curt—whom she had not seen since 1938—and his wife Ilse, and to meet her grandsons, Tom and Pete. She found work as a governess in a Jewish household and became an American citizen five years later.

Shortly after my grandmother's departure from France, we moved to a new apartment at Rue Leon Frot in the same neighbourhood. For the first time we were able to have a pet, and a black poodle called Yorick joined our small family. Yorick quickly became my closest companion.

After some time, Fred saved enough money to establish his own factory with a knitting machine to produce designs that were much in demand, while Ruth rented a shop near Place Pigale. Behind a curtain at the back of her premises was a long cutting table and a sewing machine that Ruth used to design and create the knitwear she sold in the shop. The space doubled as a changing room for customers. There was also a little kitchenette at the rear of the shop for the mandatory preparation and enjoyment of coffee and croissants.

Ruth's French identity card, 1949

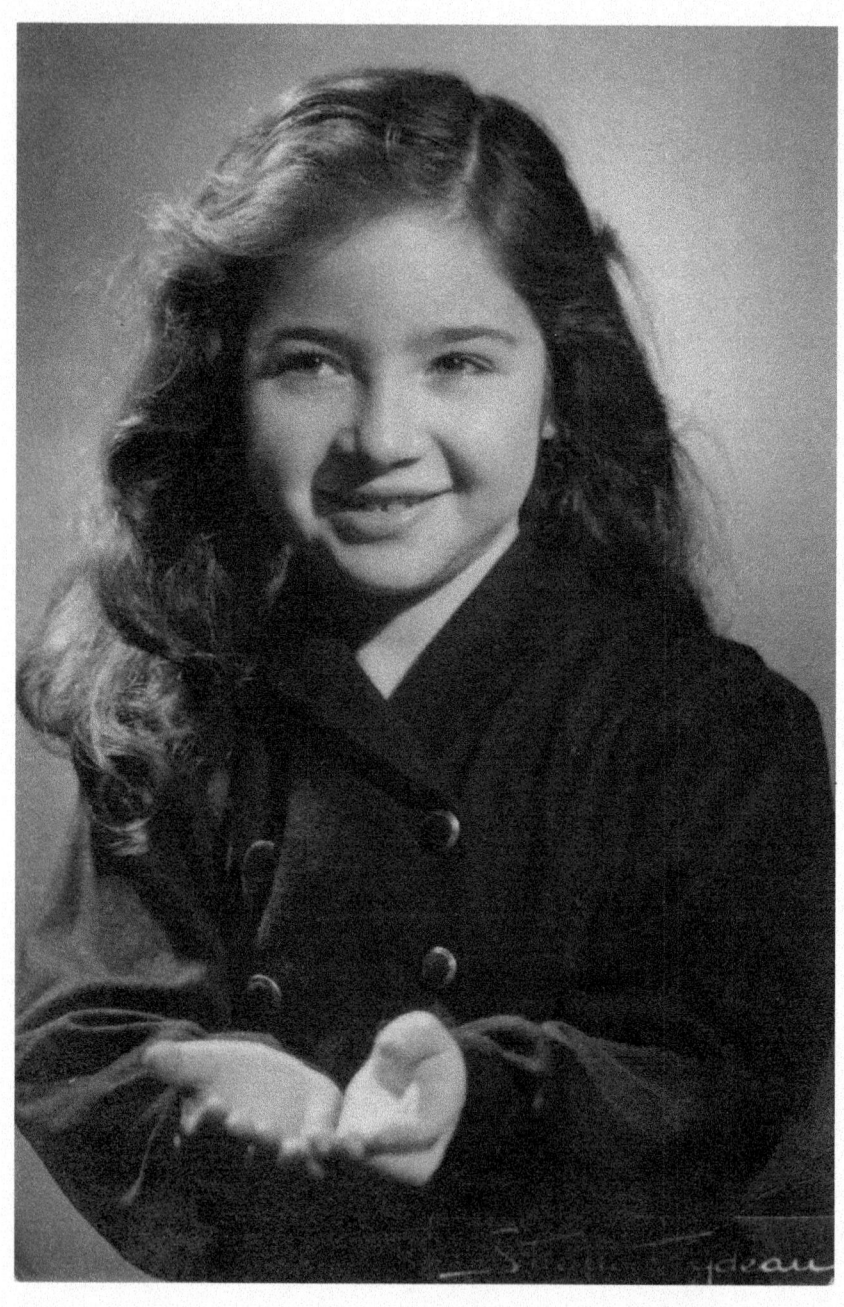

Me, c. 1948

PEACETIME

End of school year concert, June 1950

MALOU

Holidaying with friends in St Cast, Brittany, summers, 1949–1951

As Ruth and Fred worked long and irregular hours, they employed a woman to look after me each afternoon when I returned from school until my mother came home. My first nanny was an older lady named Louise, and the second, a wonderful woman called Gabrielle. They were both very wise and down to earth and I loved them dearly. I can still recall the kindness of Gabrielle as she nursed me through a bout of scarlet fever.

My parents' marriage changed rapidly during that period. After surviving the war with its many dangers, deprivations, and lengthy separations, it was not uncommon for couples to grow apart. Love fades and my parents began to drift apart. But throughout those difficult times, their love and care for me never waned.

After completing primary school, I enrolled in a highly recommended boarding school at Nogent-sur-Marne, a beautiful outer suburb of Paris. My father took me to school by car every Monday morning and I returned every Friday at noon by metro, and headed directly to my mother's shop.

Schools in France were very strict and teachers imposed rigid rules on behaviour. Many children returning to school after the enormous upheaval of their lives during the war struggled to adapt to the strict expectations of the school environment. At my boarding school, the worst punishment a teacher could give was the cancellation of weekend leave, either for an individual or, worse, an entire year group. This warning was made to the whole school assembly at the start of every week. The threat of not being able to return home to see my parents at the weekend upset me terribly and I cried every Monday morning at the beginning of the school week. That was a most unhappy time in my life.

This memorial is a prominent feature on the wall of my primary school in Paris: "Dedicated to the memories of the students of this school deported from 1942–44 because they were Jews, innocent victims of barbaric Nazis and of the Vichy Government. More than 1200 children of the 11th arrondissement were exterminated in the death camps."

The harshness of the school system contrasted greatly with the OSE which continued its work rehabilitating displaced children. The OSE recognised that many children had endured unimaginable suffering and needed all the attention, assistance and compassion that its social workers could provide.

***

While rebuilding our fractured lives, my family, like many others in the immediate post-war years, began the search for lost relatives. A colleague from the OSE advised Ruth in the search for her only surviving relative, a second cousin called Paul Stein who had migrated from Austria to Australia just prior to the war in 1938. Paul and Ruth had been playmates as young children in Vienna. Their parents had also been very close and, tragically, were all deported together on the same transport to Riga in 1942.

After my mother placed an advertisement in Australian newspapers, a friend alerted Paul that a French woman was searching for him. He was overwhelmed when he discovered that the French woman was, in fact, his Austrian cousin Ruth. They immediately began a correspondence, which in turn led to my mother making the best decision of our lives. We would leave war-shattered Europe and move to Australia to make a new start.

At the end of February 1952, to my great surprise, my headmistress informed me that I was leaving the school immediately and permanently for a trip abroad with my family.

I was delighted to find out that before immigrating to Australia, my father was taking me on a three-week trip to the United States to meet my American family and to spend some precious time with my beloved Omi. Leaving my mother in France to organise our departure to Australia, my father and I boarded the *Queen Elizabeth* for the five-day transatlantic journey from Cherbourg to New York. What followed was a fun holiday, the memory of which I will always cherish as it was the last trip I ever took with my father.

***

Paul had organised three Australian visas for our family but due to unforeseen business complications, in the weeks before we were due to leave, Fred decided to postpone his emigration.

On 16 May 1952, my mother and I bid an emotional farewell to my father at the station, and we embarked on the journey on our own. We travelled by train and ferry to London where we boarded P&O's *Oronsay* for our four-week sea voyage to Melbourne.

Once again, Ruth demonstrated her great courage and fortitude. Alone with a 12-year-old child and little English, she turned her back on the tragedies and unhappiness of the past, to start a new life on the other side of the world.

Omi, 1952

With Yorick, 1952

An outing to Coney Island with my father & grandmother, 1952

PEACETIME

Visiting my family in the US, Tom, Ilse, Curt, Omi & Peter (front), 1952

Ruth, 1956

AUSTRALIA

On our journey we met delightful travellers, many of whom were English migrants hoping to build new lives in Australia. They helped turn the trip into a special holiday. We traveled via the Suez Canal to Cairo, Aden and Ceylon[23] before reaching the west coast of Australia. I thought we had arrived in the Wild West when I saw a man carrying a Gladstone bag, just like in the western movies I had seen.

It was a cold winter's day on 18 June 1952, when, with great excitement, we sailed into Melbourne. Waving to us from the shore was my mother's cousin Paul, along with other cousins, uncles and aunties, all related to us through Leo and Margaret Altmann, my mother's parents. They were the last surviving remnants of our family[24] and it was the warmest gathering we could have imagined. That day marked the beginning of the best years of our lives.

Two days later, we gathered at the home of the oldest members of our family, Aunt Ada and Uncle Victor (Zilbermann), to celebrate our first ever shabbat. It was a very moving experience

---

23. Now Sri Lanka.

24. Paul had assisted each of these family members, like us, with immigration requirements, accommodation and employment.

for my mother and for me. In the following years, every Friday after school, I would go directly to their tiny flat in East Melbourne to help with the shabbat preparations.

When Ruth and I first arrived in Melbourne, we sublet a room in East Brighton, sharing the kitchen and bathroom with another couple. After four weeks we rented a divided house in North Brighton, which had a large common garden that we shared with our lovely Italian neighbours.

On the first Monday of our arrival, Ruth began work at a factory and I started school. With Paul's detailed written instructions, we ventured out, my mother by bus and myself on a tram. Everyone I met on the way was so friendly and helpful and the excitement of this new beginning reduced any anxiety I may have otherwise felt.

I had been warmly welcomed at Mac.Robertson Girls' High School in an interview with the principal, Miss Gainsford. The physics teacher, who also taught French with fairly basic language skills, and one of her year 12 students, were asked to sit in on the interview to interpret. It was a humorous experience for us all.

Miss Gainsford was a woman of great compassion and understanding, especially regarding the financial plight of migrant families. She did not insist, for example, that we acquire the school uniform immediately. I was embarrassed, however, to be the only student amongst all those uniform-clad girls to be wearing a tailored skirt over matching slacks with a jacket—a French winter custom—and most relieved when someone kindly offered me a second-hand uniform.

Finally settled at school, I began to make treasured, lifelong friendships for the first time. I will always remember those school years with great fondness.

From our first day in Australia, my mother and I were determined to integrate and adapt to our new life. We practiced speaking English whenever we could, listened to the radio and

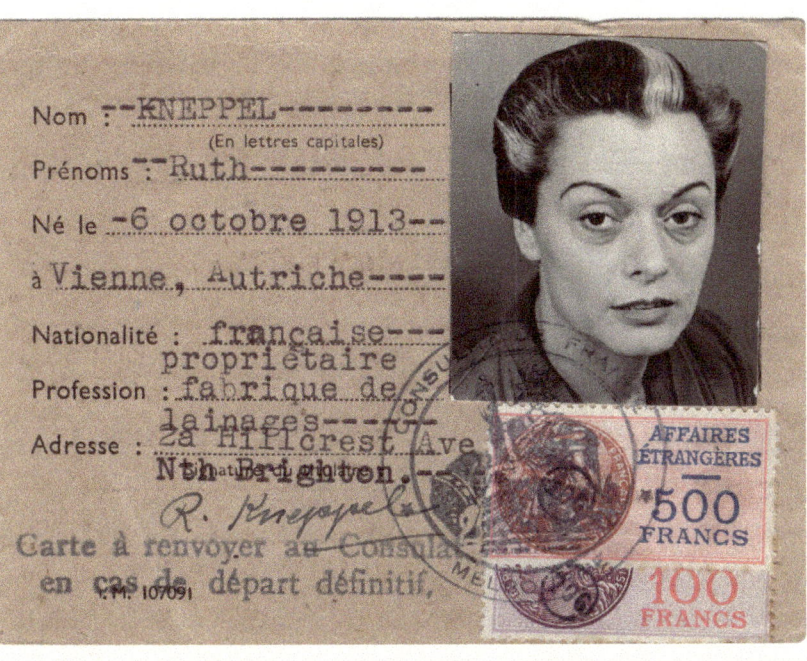

Ruth's French departure card

read newspapers. After about six months we had mastered enough English to make ourselves understood. I also began to understand German by listening to the conversations of my extended family. Throughout my childhood in France, German had never been spoken in my presence.

Although my grades were good, for financial reasons, I left school at the end of year 11 to enter Zercho's, a business college. The skills I learnt at college gave me great satisfaction and later proved valuable in my work in the clothing and fashion industry, as well as in the management of family finances.

In 1953, my father Fred was still in France and my parents made the amicable decision that it was time to get a divorce. By then, Ruth had left the factory after a few weeks and established herself in the knitwear industry. Paul and his business partner, Fred Rogers, provided Ruth with some space in the premises of their women's sportswear business, Styro, so that she could produce knitted garments under the brand 'Michèle de Lys'. For over 25 years she worked for various well-known companies such as Maglia, Exacto, and Crestknit as head knitwear designer.

A great love had blossomed between my mother and Paul, and I was delighted when they married on 7 May 1954. It was a simple civil ceremony witnessed by an intimate gathering of eight family members and friends.

My father also remarried, a French woman named Yetta. Later in 1954, Fred and Yetta, by then expecting a baby, decided that it was time to leave France. Once again, Paul assisted in arranging visas, accommodation and employment and I was thrilled to welcome the family to Melbourne. A few weeks after they arrived, to my great delight, their little girl, Vicki, was born. My grandmother Omi also decided to immigrate to Melbourne from the US to spend more time with me, my father and his new wife and child. Sadly, Omi died a few years later in 1961.

AUSTRALIA

My mother was so happy to marry Paul Stein in Melbourne, 1954

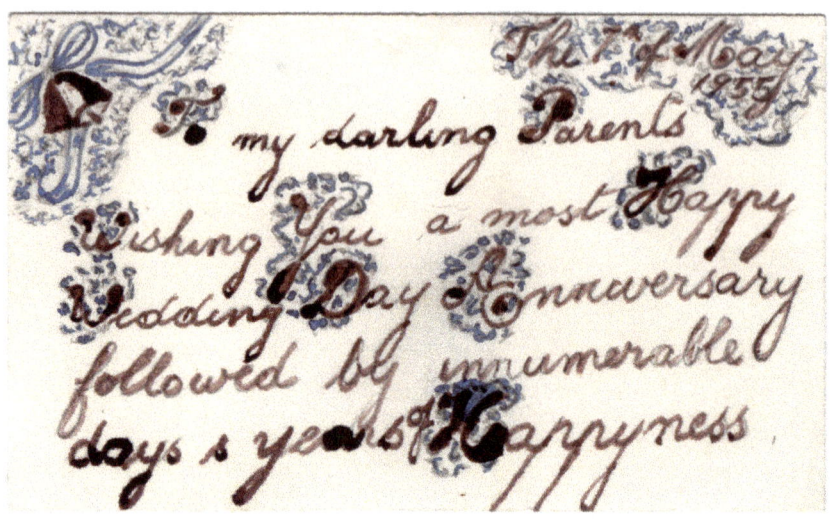

I wrote this card to congratulate my mother and Paul on their wedding day

AUSTRALIA

With my mother & stepfather at their wedding dinner, 1954

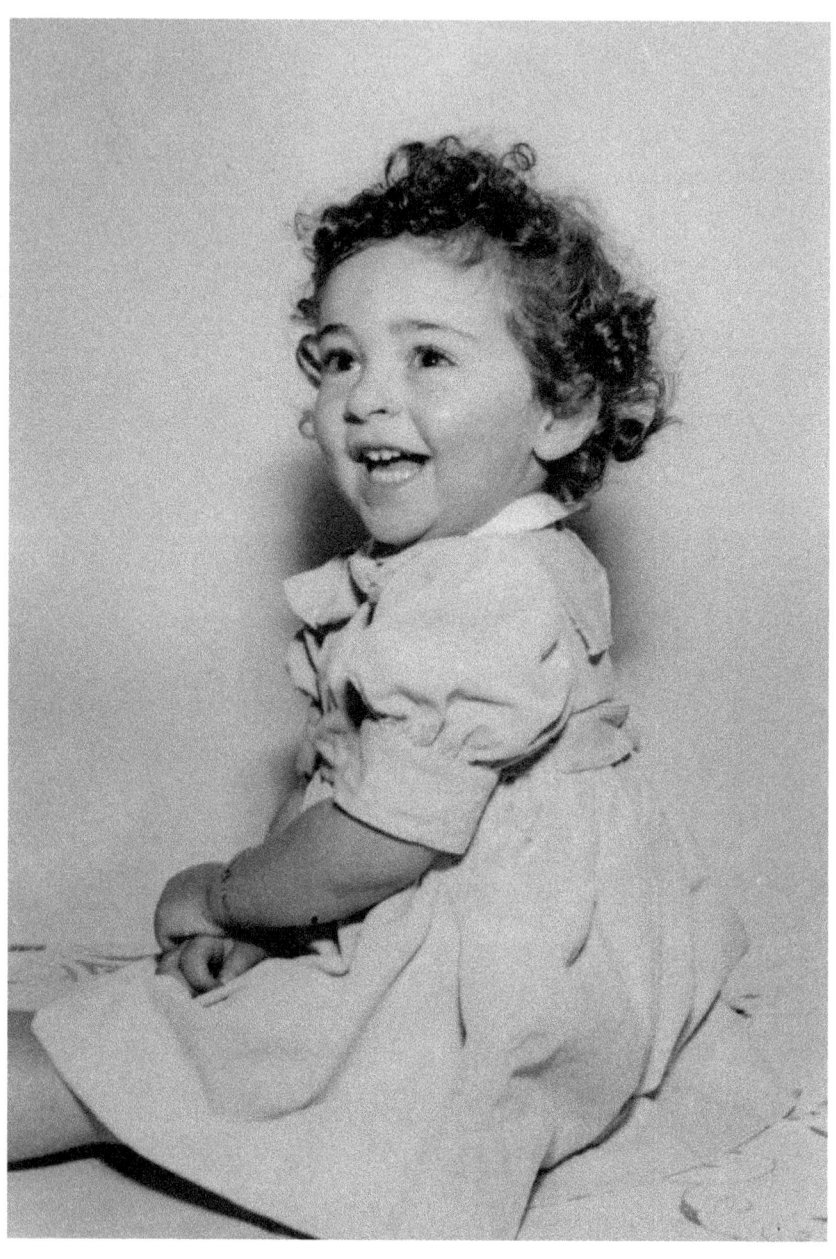

My half-sister Vicki, 1956

After first arriving in Melbourne, Fred continued to work as a knitting specialist. He later managed a general store, and eventually found great job satisfaction as a representative for a large condiments company called Hoyts.

In June 1960, I met the love of my life, Paul Huppert, a most remarkable and positive man. Paul had immigrated to Australia from Czechoslovakia, arriving in Melbourne on Australia Day in 1950.

Paul had miraculously survived the Holocaust; he spent two years in the ghetto-labour camp Theresienstadt before being transported to Auschwitz-Birkenau. By the end of the war, he was imprisoned at Kaufering, a satellite work camp of Dachau where, tragically, his older brother Kurt died, aged 15, on 3 January 1945.

After he was liberated by the Americans in April 1945, Paul, aged just 13 years old, travelled to his family's designated rendezvous address in Prague, in the hope that he would be reunited with his mother, Lene, and his stepfather, Franta. A neighbour informed him that his parents had indeed survived, and that Franta had gone to collect Lene who been liberated from the Bergen-Belsen concentration camp in northern Germany. They had no idea that Paul was alive and were overjoyed to be reunited with him on their return. By the time the family arrived in Australia three years later, Paul also had a two-year-old sister Eva.

After a whirlwind courtship, Paul and I married on 12 December 1960. We were married for 38 blissful years and during that time we were blessed with three wonderful children, Debbie, David and Tommy, their spouses Steven, Leonie and Yasmin, and the first five of our 11 grandchildren.

After a short break from work to have a family, I was asked, in 1972, to help establish a second kindergarten at the North Eastern Jewish War Memorial Centre in Doncaster. It was supposed to be a short-term position, but I found working with children and interacting with parents so enjoyable that I ended up staying in the role for 12 years. After leaving, I resumed my business interests.

Paul Huppert, 1979

Celebrating my mother's 80th birthday at the Hilton, 1993

ABOVE: Ruth & Paul Stein, 1993
BELOW: Paul & Ruth with their granchildren and spouses Steven, Debbie, David, Leonie, Tommy & Yasmin

When, at 65, Paul became ill, he retired from CSIRO where he had enjoyed a career as senior electronic engineer and chief scientist in the electronics division of mineral physics. At that time, I began to take over the administration of our personal affairs and the affairs of my elderly parents. Paul died on 21 December 1999, my 60th birthday. Two years later, in 2001, my father also passed away.[25]

After Paul's death, my business background became my lifeline to personal endurance and independence. Undoubtedly my independent spirit is a trait I inherited from Malou.

After three years alone, Eric Taft AO, a widower and highly respected dermatologist, quietly entered my life and we began a 17-year partnership. We had both already been blessed with wonderful marriages and considered this partnership a 'second chance' that neither of us had ever expected. Most remarkable and fulfilling was the immediate, wonderful bond that continues to exist between our two families, the Tafts and Hupperts.

***

Although I am officially a Holocaust survivor, I have always found it hard to accept this label. In my mind, it belongs to survivors such as my parents, Omi, Paul, his mother and stepfather, and my many friends and acquaintances whose suffering became deeply etched in their souls. I consider myself to have been blessed that, throughout that war period, my amazing mother was able to provide me with exceptional protection and care. She also ensured that I was surrounded with love and security throughout my life.

---

25. My half-sister Vicki married Mark Thomson and they had four daughters, including triplets. After my father died, Yetta moved into a retirement village close to Vicki and her family, where she continued her passion in gardening and knitting beautiful items for her grandchildren until she passed away peacefully in 2016.

With Eric, 2003

AUSTRALIA

With my grandchildren, 2013

After defying the Nazis and enduring the devastation of the war in Europe, Ruth and Paul lived a long and happy life in Australia. They enjoyed 50 wonderful years of marriage and treasured their role as 'Nunny' and 'Bah' to their three grandchildren and six great-grandchildren. Their full life included supporting Israel, involvement with the Jewish organisations B'nai B'rith and Women's International Zionist Organization (WIZO), and much travel. Treasured friendships had a special place in their hearts. Their love and devotion for each other, and family, was boundless. Sadly, my stepfather, Paul Stein, died in 2004.

Ruth's elegance, charm, pride, dignity and courage never left her. In one of her final interviews, in the autumn of her life, Ruth declared that, looking back on her work with the Resistance, she could still not believe what she had managed to achieve.

My beautiful brave mother died in Melbourne on 6 June 2007.

Ruth, 2004

ACKNOWLEGEMENTS

I approached the Jewish Holocaust Centre in Melbourne in search of a permanent home for Ruth's precious documents in the hope they would be preserved and shared, and that Malou's activities as a female partisan in World War II would be given due recognition. The response from senior archivist Dr Anna Hirsh was overwhelmingly positive and she urged me to write my mother's story. It took several months to gather my courage but, when I did finally put pen to paper, vivid memories from my early life were awoken and, in the process, I learned more about myself as well as about my mother's life. Writing this book has been a labour of love and I am greatly indebted to Anna for believing in me. I thank her profoundly.

In 2018, when browsing through a bookshop in Melbourne, I was attracted to the title of the book *Les Parisiennes*. Reading this wonderful book invoked the world of my past! The author, Anne Sebba, evocatively depicts the lives of women in Paris during World War II. She describes many of the journeys my mother undertook, including her 1939 escape northward, and our return journey by road to Paris in 1940 under heavy bombardment. *Les Parisiennes* filled in gaps in my knowledge of precise dates and events, and other details missing from my early childhood memories. I immediately sent Anne an email to convey the profound impact her book had on me. She replied and over time we have become good friends. The accidental discovery of Anne's work provided further motivation for the writing of this book and I am so very grateful to her.

Around the same time, I became acquainted online with Danielle Darquié, a French historian and writer with a particular interest in the work of the Resistance movement in the Dordogne region. We corresponded and Danielle kindly assisted with my research into my mother's past. I am eternally grateful that Danielle posted me a copy of her book, *Dans les pas des Resistants (In the steps of the Resistants)* which traces all aspects of the Resistance work in Lot-et-Garonne from Fumel to Lemance, and throughout France. It is an intensely researched and exceptionally detailed book, which I found fascinating.

In January 2020, I received the second edition of Danielle's book, the title of which translates to: *In the steps of the Resistants along the shores of the (river) Lot*. In this most detailed edition, Danielle describes the lives and missions of the Resistance fighters and the groups they formed. There is also a section dedicated to women in the war. Of particular significance to me are the chapters focusing on Villeveuve-sur-Lot and my mother's Resistance group, Prosper. My mother is featured in a group photograph of Prosper and is mentioned in several passages:

> Ruth Kneppel, together with Jane Kayser, both Jewish, participated equally in the creation of Union des Femmes Francaises of Villeneuve.

> [In Prosper]...a group of young girls and women, which included Ruth Kneppel, played a major role as couriers, liaison agents and nurses in the liberation of Agen in the Dordogne.

But most poignant to me is the chapter headed, 'The Journeys of Ruth Altmann Kneppel, Austrian Resistance Fighter', which has been invaluable for the writing of this book.

I was delighted to facilitate contact between Anne Sebba and Danielle Darquié as I felt their research was complementary. I believe they remain in touch and I sincerely hope that I will one day meet both amazing women in person.

To Anne, Danielle and Anna, you have all been so generous with your time and your friendship. I am eternally grateful to you all for your unconditional dedication to my project when you yourselves are so occupied with you own research. I cannot thank you enough.

To my publisher, Real Film & Publishing, my deep appreciation for accepting this project. My gratitude goes to Georgie Raik-Allen, with whom I worked closely, as well as Romy Moshinsky, for their guidance, patience and professionalism in assisting me in the production of this very special book.

***

To Eric Taft, my partner whom I lost in November 2019. Eric so enjoyed my parents' company. He is the one who first suggested, when we were planning a trip to France in 2011, that we should visit the places of my childhood. And we did! That trip, together with the discovery of my mother's war documents, inspired my journey into Malou's past. I remain forever grateful that Eric propelled me with those first early steps towards writing this book.

To David, my son, who, with gentle persuasion, encouraged my mother and her husband Paul, already in their late 80s, to finally agree to give videoed testimonies to Phillip Maisel, OAM,

ACKNOWLEDGEMENTS

at the Jewish Holocaust Centre. Buried in the depth of her mind, my mother recalled many painful memories which she would have preferred to lay to rest. With great strength and dignity, she shared stories of her life which were so valuable to me in writing this book. David, you also found precious time to assist me with numerous technical issues. I thank you most sincerely.

I owe my deepest appreciation to two of my granddaughters. Judy, for designing the 1940–1944 map of France, and her sister Dinah, who has taken charge of publicity for this book.

To Leonie, my daughter-in-law, thank you for translating *IVRIA Recollections* using special technology, and for digitising all the images that appear in this book. I am profoundly grateful and appreciative, especially as you dedicated your time for this project during a particularly busy period in your own work schedule.

To my other children, Debbie and her husband Steven, Tommy and his wife Yasmin. You all adored your unique grandmother and I thank you for encouraging me to persevere with this emotional task.

innigsten Glückwünsche wollen
nächsten Sagen nachlagen. Hoffent-
... hier doch wohl will zu das ne-
... ein und einige ...
... so vorgemischt mit ist, ...
... vielen ... Dokumenten ...
nicht ... sondern weiter ...
... deren ... wie ...
... nach ... dieses Früh-
... glauben wird. ...
Oft denke ich daran, wenn soll ich ...
... dann jeder Mensch sich zu ...
und sich von Gott zu ...
... wundern, auch ob ... über ...
... oder in einer Dezember ...
... besuchen ... das Kind ...
... habe und wird als ...
... fest und voller Gottes ...
bei euch. Gott sei die l. Kleinen ...
... frohen Herzen im ...
auch ... Gottes natürlich. ...
... und Schutz wird. — Wir ...
den letzten ...

APPENDICES

APPENDIX A

Letters sent to Ruth in Paris from her parents, Leo and Margaret, in Vienna, 1939–1941

Dear beloved children,

Do not rely on anyone, be careful when taking orders, and do not make calculations too modest. Do not join a campaign team, but rather gather your strengths for when the work is urgent. As a foreigner, do not interfere in politics. Do not sympathise with the left or the right, take the straight path, that is to say the Jewish line! Such types as the communists …… have engendered Hitlerism ……. and anti-Semitism in Germany; they have of course not believed with their political stupidity that Hitler will come one day. The same thing can happen in France. You are still young, think carefully about whether you should undertake the planned trip to Chamonix? Or to Vienna? Everything costs money, maybe you're better off better relaxing there! I hope to visit you again in a short time, that is to say, if I stay in good health.

Dear beloved children! Dear little child Michi!

Your little darling birthday is approaching, and I am sending you a small gift for a beautiful new teddy bear or whatever. We want to send you our most sincere congratulations and to implore God's richest blessings for you. I hope we will still have…the pleasure of writing you for your birthday.

But if you do not receive from us (correspondence) for a few weeks, do not despair, because it is possible that we too will soon be resettled like so many other acquaintances. But we are not disturbed, as we continue to be courageous and full of confidence in God. He is everywhere. We still think and we hope that we will have a happy reunion somewhere after the end of this terrible war. We must be as good as possible, because every human being must be ready to be called and to be justified before God.

To look at you again, to be able to kiss the child again, it is our hopeful prayer and it will remain wherever we are. Continue to be steady and confident in God; we are always with you in our thoughts. Warmly greet your beloved dear parents, hug and kiss little Fratz again and again. We take your little picture with us, as well as your photos of course.

Michi smiles at us with so much love that it warms our hearts. We have had and still have enough agitation in recent weeks with the departure of many good acquaintances. As long as we can stay here, we want to write to you quite often, every week at least one card. Aunt Resi and Uncle Ludwig are still here, thank God. Lotte could be in Poznana in the labour department just like other people who can work, while her parents should be with the elderly in Lodz. I do not want to write much, the letter has to leave.

My beloved ones, always remain good and diligent as before, may God bless you and protect you from all evil and danger. Never forget, if you have a good conscience.... all the inconveniences are easier to bear. Today you are still young.... We are calm and completely devoted to God, do not worry about us, we do not despair, even if we have to leave. We would be grateful and happy if we could stay here for the winter until spring, but why would we be better off than so many others? When you write again, be very careful.

God bless you! Your dear old mother.

Stay healthy and be brave!
I kiss you and I am your faithful dad.

Dear beloved children,

We do not know how much to report. As soon as we receive mail again from you, we will write to you in more detail. Are you healthy? What does our little darling do? Please write immediately.

Greetings to you all and many kisses,
your mum and dad.

Warm greetings and kisses, Papa

Ruth's parents, Leo & Margaret Altmann

Dear little Michi!

Your first birthday is approaching. We can only send you our most sincere congratulations and blessings in writing. May God protect you and preserve you in every way. I caress your dear head in my imagination and your dear parents and grandparents should give you many, many kisses from us and show you our pictures. We are always with you in our thoughts, you know it; we hope that the beloved God will let us meet again one day, ….. with you it will be a first meeting.

Stay healthy, wise and dear as in your first year of life and, until you understand it, follow the example of your dear, good, diligent and modest parents.

The photos of you and your beloved parents are in front of me on the table. I cannot believe you're such a great lady. We are very proud of you, little Kitzerle. And infinitely grateful to God that you look so splendid. Your dear mother is also very beautiful and, on the next picture, we believe we can also see your dear Papa. We allow ourselves to enlarge the beautiful images, which gave us infinite joy, of course. Of course, we have been looking at your photos for a long time with the magnifying glass and our glasses.

To whom, little Fratzerl, you will resemble, we cannot say yet, it will be seen later. Your mother had a face so round and arms so thick, only the hair was not so beautiful. Peter was also such a bullet and your uncle Kurt must have looked like that. Anyway, you're a pretty kid, smart, sweet, tall, strong and healthy, that's the main thing. God make your parents always have joy with you, and become a good and wise person, and always be in good health.

In one of the photographs it looks like you have just eaten spinach or chocolate. Do you already have a dear teddy bear who is loved above all else? I often see beautiful toys that you would like too. But for today only, once again, my most intimate congratulations from my heart, and many kisses to your dear parents and your other grandparents.

Your Omama, who loves you a lot.

P.S. We have now received your letter of July 30 and we see that our great concern for you was not unjustified. Thank God, you are now in your house and you have forgotten all the difficulties. Keep wise and healthy, dear God will already give us a goodbye. I do not need to make sure our thoughts are always with you. We are very happy that the little one is well hardened and that she eats everything so well. All our acquaintances love the picture of our little Michi.

My dear Esti-Michi!

Since we are in possession of your photos and those of your dear mother, our modest house has had a festive atmosphere that raises us above the worries of everyday life. My joy would be great if, as a grandfather, I could squeeze my little Uzi Mutzi Putzi to congratulate you on your first birthday. Dear Omama has thought of you on this occasion with so many heartfelt congratulations that I have almost nothing to say, but I would like to add a wish: that you, dear Mischinko, come into the world under the sign of the god Mars, that the angel of peace keeps you and protects the happy days of you and your dear parents.

My dear loved ones!

Dear little sweet Michi, we wish you, our darling, all the best for your birthday. May the good Lord bless you and look after you! This year you are already a big girl and you will understand when your dear parents and dear grandparents will give you many kisses also on behalf of your distant grandparents. We can only in our imagination caress your sweet little face and look at the photograph that is smiling at us from the frame on the wall. We only ask the dear Lord to let you grow to become a pretty and well-behaved, good girl. We already expressed our birthday wishes in the previous letter, but we think that these lines will reach you before your birthday.

At the same time, we would like to thank you dear children for the two parcels, which were delivered by mail. The shoes are wonderful, they fit well and fulfil their purpose and Papa is very happy with the style and quality and has cleaned and polished them in the usual manner. And I am happy that I do not have

APPENDICES

Letters sent from my grandparents in Vienna marked with the postage stamp of the Nazi regime

to wear new shoes, but that I am wearing shoes that you, dear Ruth, have softened before. However, the thought worries me that you yourself could have worn these good ..... shoes still for a long time. I am wearing the cardigan underneath a sleeveless dress and so it fits perfectly, is warm and I have a good addition to the dress which until now I was not able to wear, because I did not have a blouse to wear underneath. I already boiled the fat; it is very delicious, just like the pasta. But enough now about the presents, dear children. Don't worry, we are healthy, and of course you know that we always think of you. Is the little one not coughing anymore? We have already had very cold days and snow, but now it is nice and warm, almost too warm, which is not healthy for this time of year. Did you have a cold already, dear Fritz? I already had a cold and used up many paper tissues. What are your dear parents doing? What about Aunt Rosa? Aunt .... wrote us today, she has not received any mail from Maria in quite some time, and she also told us that Aunt Ella and Uncle Ignaz moved house, but their new address is unknown so far. Whether this information is true, we do not know, since only a couple of days ago we received a card from Aunt Ella from their old address. As Aunt Rosa told us, however, from the next week they will live in a small summer residence which Papa and I still remember from when we were young. Did you already get together with the son of our neighbours? He has in the meantime written to his parents. Write soon how you are doing. Once again, our sincerest wishes and warmest regards and kisses to all of you. I embrace you.

Yours, Mammi

Dear sweet Esti-Michèle,

Today you are the main topic of our letter, because you are quickly approaching your second birthday and your grandparents who live far away would like to congratulate you. Time is passing so quickly that I have to ask myself today, how come you are already celebrating your second birthday, my sweet angel. I still remember the long hours when, for a period of almost two weeks, we were waiting for the telegram to tell us about the arrival of the baby, and now, dear little girl, you have become a little lady, who is smiling cheekily from the photograph on the wall, filling us with hope of a happy reunion!

May your days, which God will grant you, be as carefree and happy as your smile, my little angel, making your parents happy, your parents who are caring for you in good times and in bad times.

This is my deepest wish, which I include in my daily prayer!

Dear Fritz and dear Ruti, as always, I wish you all the best as well. Stay brave, energetic and hard-working. Kind regards to Ernie and Frieda. I would be happy to hear from them.

I embrace and kiss you,

Your faithful father

APPENDIX B

Testimonies

Hand-written letter
Prosper commandant Marcel Langer
1 September 1944

I certify that Madame R Kneppel was in the ranks of my company since the month of March 1943 and left once all the missions I gave her were completed. She left my company in September 1944.

M Langer, commandant of battalion Prosper

Ordre de Mission,
Commandant de la place de Villeneuve-sur-Lot, FFI
23 December 1944

Valid to leave 24 December 1944

Madame Kneppel Ruth (non de guerre Malou) responsible for the Union des Femmes Francais of Villeneuve is sent on a mission to Nice for propaganda business. This *order de mission* is priority for the return to Villeneuve-sur-Lot and valid for one month.

Order to accord her the utmost facilities possible.

En campagne
Le 1er Septembre 1944

Je certifie que Madame R. Knobel a été dans les rangs de ma compagnie depuis le mois de mars 1943 et qu'elle a rempli toutes les missions que je lui ai demandées. Elle a quitté ma compagnie au mois de septembre 1944.

Le Capitaine Bataillon Prosper

Testimony
Captain Ferdinand Gaumy
19 March 1945

I, the undersigned, Gaumy Ferdinand, Commandant of the Instruction Company de L'Ecole de Cadres, Chief of the Resistance of the Interior of the Central 12 d'Elysees, certify with honor to have employed Madame Ruth Kneppel as agent of liaison from January 1943 till February 1944. She was continuously in contact with political detainees, in assuring them of arms and food, always discharging her work with *sang-froid* and courage. With perfect knowledge of the German language, we were able to obtain information on the enemy on the way to our town, information always exact and often of the greatest importance. She exemplified, whatever the circumstances, such audacity and *sang-froid* worthy of all commendation."

CONSEIL NATIONAL DE LA RÉSISTANCE
COMMISSION MILITAIRE
(ex-Comac)

M⁻ Malau ou KNEPPEL qualité FFI
Villeneuve s/lot
porter l'insigne F. F. I., N° 184.619, est autorisé à attestant sa participation effective aux combats de la Libération.
Autorité certifiant de l'authenticité des titres du porteur de l'insigne :
Le Chancelier :
Les Commissaires

Ecole des Cadres
de Castelialoux.

ATTESTATION

Je soussigné GAUMY Fernand Capitaine Commandant la Compagnie d'instruction de l'Ecole deCadres, ancien chef de la resistance interieure de la Centrale d'Eysses, certifie sur l'honneur avoir employé comme agent de liaison Madame Ruth KNEPPEL du mois de Janvier 1943 au mois de Fevrier 1944. Elle a été continuellement en contact avec les détenus politiques, assurant leurs ravitaillement en-armes, munitions et avitaillement, elle s'est toujours acquittée de son travail avec sang-froid et courage.
Sa connaissance parfaite de la langue Allemande, nous a permis d'obtenir des renseignements sur l'ennemi lors de son passage dans notre ville, renseignements toujours exacts et de la plus haute importance
Elle a fait preuve en n'importe quelle circonstance d'une audace et d'un sang-froid digne de tout age.

Casteljaloux 19 mars 1945

Le Capitaine MY
Commandant la Compagnie
d'instruction l'Ecole
des Cadres
Ancien chef de Resistance
interieure de Centrale d'Eysses.

Reference
Union des Femmes Francaises delegate, Simone Papon
3 March 1945

I, the undersigned, Simone Papon, delegate of the Union des Femmes Francaise in the department of Liberation of the Lot-et-Garonne, certify that Ruth Kneppel worked for the Resistance, transporting arms under the nose of the Germans.

I can confirm that she has done everything possible in her power to hasten the liberation of France, thus repaying back the debt of recognition to the Nation who welcomed her.

At the liberation of Villeneuve-sur-Lot, whilst the Germans were still in the town, she participated in one of the most active, and fastest growing groups of the Committee of the l'Union des Femmes Francaise, therefore she was nominated in charge until she left. She directed this Resistance movement with great intelligence and tact, bringing to the authorities her influence and a most precious collaboration to resolve all serious problems of the hour.

Je soussignée PAPON Simone, Déléguée de l'UNION DES FEMMES FRANÇAISES, au Comité Départemental de Libération de Lot-et-Garonne certifie avoir rencontré Madame KNEPPEL Ruth, en novembre 1943 alors qu'elle travaillait pour la Résistance transportant, plis, armes, etc.. au nez des boches.

Je puis affirmer qu'elle a fait toutce qui était en son pouvoir pour hâter la libération de la France, payant ainsi la dette de reconnaissance à la Nation qui l'avait accueillie.

Dès la libération de Villeneuve-sur-Lot, alors que les Allemands étaient encore dans le Lot-et-Garonne, elle a participé d'une façon des plus actives à l'élargissement du Comité de l'Union des Femmes Françaises, dont elle a été nommée responsable et où elle est restée jusqu'à son départ. Elle a dirigé ce Mouvement de Résistance avec beaucoup d'intelligence et de tact apportant aux Pouvoirs Publics tout son appui et une collaboration des plus précieuses pour résoudre tous les graves problèmes de l'heure.

Agen, le 3 mars 1945.

Memo
OSE director general, Madame Andre Salomon
18 April 1945

Dear Madam,

I would like to add a few favourable words to assist with the enquiry of Madame Ruth Kneppel, who is one of my oldest friends. I know her particularly well and if I can be a moral guarantor, I can also confirm the validity of her curriculum vitae; her experience tells me she certainly would be a most valued worker for OSE.

Very sincerely, Andree Salomon

Letter
OSE colleague, J Samuel

August 1946

We sincerely regret that your personal situation has led you to stop your precious collaboration with our Bureau. We have followed with great interest your work since you commenced on 1 June 1945 and noted all your efforts and results that you obtained.

We hope that you will keep in contact with work and your colleagues and we all wish you the best for the future and your family.

APPENDICES

AMERICAN JOINT DISTRIBUTION COMMITTEE
OFFICE FOR FRANCE
19, AVENUE FOCH
PARIS (16ᵉ)

CABLES & TELEGRAMS
JOINTFUND-PARIS

TÉLÉPHONES
PASSY 53-51
35-29

June 4, 1946

Paris General Letter #58

To : A.J.D.C. Vienna

From: A.J.D.C. Paris

Subj: Mrs. Ruth Käeppel

Gentlemen:

    This will introduce Mrs. Ruth Käeppel, an employee of OSE, France, who has come to Vienna on OSE business. We would appreciate any assistance you may be able to give Mrs. Käeppel in carrying out her work, and in the matter of housing and maintenance for her during her stay in Vienna.

Yours truly,

Auren Kahn
Acting Director Program for France

AK/es

-143-

APPENDIX C
IVRIA

It is not possible to write a complete history of the IVRIA but a brief account should serve as a reminder of key events and people dear to all members, as well as recognising the small but important role of IVRIA in Zionist history.

IVRIA was formed in 1871 with the name Association of Austrian-Silesian High School Students. It was a Zionist group of young people passionate about Theodor Herzl and his ideas. Initially it included both non-Jews and Jews as members. Eventually, however, the non-Jews decided to form their own group and IVRIA became a solely Jewish organisation. The process was civil and for decades IVRIA members maintained friendly relations with their non-Jewish brothers.

IVRIA members came mostly from Moravia, Frydek-Mistek and Vienna. As the World Zionist Organization membership from Russia to Central Europe increased considerably IVRIA headquarters moved from Vienna to Cologne, Germany.

Many IVRIA members took part in the First Zionist Conference in Basel, Switzerland in August 1897. Two other organisations were also represented at the conference, Kadima, which had formed 10 years earlier, and Unitas.

The last general meeting of the IVRIA took place in Moravia on 1 November 1937. Months later, Hitler marched into Austria. Many Jews were deported and died. Those who survived migrated to Palestine, then Israel in 1949 and to various countries throughout the world including Australia.

IVRIA FOUNDATION MEMBERS
As documented at the IVRIA 80th anniversary celebrations in Israel, 1971

Dr Louis Poborski (Pagat) Died Vienna
Eng Emil Fried (Frosch) Died Theresienstadt
Dr Benno Hahn (Cooq) Died Tel Aviv
Dr Julius Kohn (Cujus) Died Maehr Ostrau
Eng Philipp Singer (Mond) Died Polen
Prof Klitz (Klitz) Died Teschen
Eng Hahn (Bacchus) Died Vienna
Dr Max Kleinberg (Weichselzopf) Died Polen
Dr Karl Kohn (Mnelik) Died Theresienstadt
Dr Arnold Colbi (Arnold) Died Tel Aviv
Dr Alex Friedman (Pax)
Dr Benno Schallinger (Benno) Died Kiriat Chaim
Dr Antonio Colbi (Toni) Died Triest
Eng Hugo Wertheim (Wertheim) Died New York
Dr Alfred Lanzer (Reddy) Died Tel Aviv
Philipp Ruebenstein (Philipp) Died Theresienstadt
Dr Edmund Weizmann (Eddo) Died Vienna
Architect Berthold Marmorstein Died Weltkrieg
Dr Eng Richard Karplus (Karplus) Died New York
Dr Arthur Immerglueck Mazel) Died London
Dr Emil Krasny (Joff) Died London
Dr Oskar Frankl (Oki) Died New York
Dr Hugo Deutsch (Archkenes) Died Theresienstadt
Dr Herbert Kurrein (Karoki) Died Haifa
Eng Karl Nachmann Died Theresiendadt
Dr Alexander Hausmann Died Lemburg
Eng Leo Altmann (Lazy)
Otto Wechsberg (Otto) Died New York
Rudolf Nassau (Maxl) Died Vienna
Dr Jakob Ehrlich (Vetter) Died Dachau
Dr Siegfried Frankl (Bentschma) Died Luhacovice

Max Kunz Died America
Dr Jaques Kornfield (Cokl)
Dr I.H.Koerner (Klofac) Died Tel Aviv
Eng Felix Zweigenthal (Phylax) Died Aushwitz
Eng Fedof Goldschneider (Fedor) Died Ostrau
Dr Adolf Lanzer (Bozzo) Died Auschwitz
Eng Julius Groag (Julius) Died Auschwitz
Eng Wilhelm Vogel (Vogel) Died Vienna
Dr Hugo Lowi (Nathan) Died England
Dr Oscar Nassau (Oscar) Died Aushwitz
Dr Albert Schoenhof (Jurek) Died Weltkrieg
Max Reicher Died Auschwitz
Richard Fraenkel (Frook) Died Haifa
Dr Robert Beer (Petz) Died London
Dr Leopold Friedman (Paxl) Died Tel Aviv
Dr Herman Loew (Vinzenz) Died Paris
Dr Ernst Wechsberg (Ernstl) Died Auschwitz
Dip. Kaufmann Arthur Wechsberg (Kakisch) Died Auschwitz
Dr Edwin Strauss (Juja) Died Auschwitz
Eng Ernst Reinisch (Reinisch) Died Auschwitz
Dr Sal Hornung (Pschuett) Died Weltkrieg
Dr Felix Winterstein (Soci) Died Haifa
Dr Oscar Fraenkl (Froeckl) Died New York
Eng Jul Schallinger (Scholet)
Eng Otto Krasny (Joeffl) Died San Francisco
Dr Leopold Leschner (Polde) Died Venezuela
Dr Hans Schoenhof (Jureczek) Died Bruenn
Zdenko Koenigstein (Puffy) Died San Paolo
Dr Benno Binovic (Bini) Died Paris
Dr Arthur Reik (Turek) Died Tel Aviv
Dr Adolf Brand (Abesch) Died Auschwitz
Eng Oskar Presser Died America
Eng Benno Huller (Tip) Died Tel Aviv
Dr Alfred Loewenstein (Fredl) Died Tel Aviv
Dr Paul Lenk (Gyges) Died Auschwitz

Dr Ernst Horhung (Febi) Died Auschwitz
Dr Fritz Singer (Sing) Died Vienna
Dr Leo Singer (Sang) Died Aushwitz
Dr Otto Eisler (Ottek) Died Ostrau
Dr Karl Eisler (Wipfel) Died Auschwitz
Eng Fritz Lindenberger (Flix) Died Auschwitz
Eng Ernst Ruebenstain (Rips) Died Auschwitz
Adolf Gelbart (Bartl) Died Auschwitz
Ernst Roth (Korek) Died California
Eng Ernst Kaeufler (Storch) Died America
Dr Emil Mueller (Klapp) Died Haifa
Dr Richard Tuttmann (Tutti) Died Brazil
Leo Arthur Robiczek (Vinci) Died Caracas
Dr Ernst Nassau (Bonk) Died Haifa
Dr Oscar Singer (Kling) Died Auschwitz
Dr Isidor Brand (Bobesch) Died Auschwitz
Leo Schoener (Rahu) Died Tel Aviv
Dr Karl Steiner (Sigi) Died Sydney
Dr Josef Schornstein (Schlot) Died Ostrau
Richard Bender
Bidermann (Buddha) Died Bucharest
Wollak (Boga)
Dr Ferdinand Barber (Sisi) Died Auschwitz
Eng Alfred Barber (Dudu) Died Auschwitz
Eng Otto Alban-fr-Altmann (Ali) Died Melbourne
Walter Gruenwalk (Simpl) Died Prerau
Dr Bernhard Klamer (Buki) Died Israel
Dr David Paul Merez -fr-Maerz (Russ) Died Jerusalem
Dr Richard Aufricht (Fruechtl) Died New York
Dr Otto Graf (Maggi) Died Auschwitz
Arthur Singer (Klang) Died Ostrau
Dr Oscar Schnitzer (Praxel) Died London
Dr Isidor Glaser Schraml) Died Israel
Dr Berthold Gutmann (Zumpel) Died Auschwitz
Dr Maximilian Goettlinger (Goettl) Died Sao Paolo

Dr Franz Nassau (Srap) Died Tel Aviv
Paul Fulton- Foldes (Fofl) Died Haifa
Otto Loew (Reb) Died Tel Aviv
Eng Alfred Goldberger (Grinsl) Died London
Ernst Borger (Posa) Died Auschwitz
Ernst Lang (Pinkus) Died Auschwitz
Arpad Grossmann (Trepl) Died Maher Ostrau
Gustav Bock (Olla) Died Sydney
Hans Kandl (Nuche) Died Oranienburg
Dr Karl Sommer
Eng Spielmann (Srok)
Eugen Better (Pintsch) Died Tel Aviv
Josef Koeniger (Rexl) Died Israel
Max Borger (Ases) Died Tel Aviv
Dr Alfred Guen (Barry) Died New York
Dr Desider-Deszo-Weiss (Blanko) Died New York
Joseph Fraenkel (Rebbe) Died London
Dr Edmund Fraenkel (Foxl) Died England
Dr Leopold Laufer (Tobias) Died Auschwitz
Dr Robert J Mann (Wampo) Died New York
Dr Paul G Rogers (Dackl) Died England
Dr Leo Reich (Kozzi) Died London
Dr Ernst Neumann (Patsch) Died London
Ernesto Baruch (Mule) Died Trieste
Dr Abraham Nebenzahl (Clausus) Died America
Dr Ed Pachtmann (Navi) Died Tel Aviv
DR David Bukspan (Mikro) Died Tel Aviv
Dr Isidor Rubinstein (Asra) Died Tel Aviv
Dr Miklos Cserepfalvi Died America
Dr Willi Perl (Teff) Died America
Dr Abraham Kolski (Orloff) Died Tel Aviv
Dr Karl Lachovitz (Phoetus) Died Israel
Chaim Kubiczek (Hase) Died Israel
Hans Adler (Lulef) Died Vienna

APPENDIX D

OSE

L'Oeuvre de Secours des Enfants (OSE) is a humanitarian organisation, established in 1912 by doctors in Russia to assist disadvantaged members of the Jewish population. By the 1930s, it had relocated to France and narrowed its focus to the dedicated rescue and assistance of Jewish children whose parents had been imprisoned in concentration camps or murdered by the Nazis.

From the late 1930s, the OSE established a number of mansions throughout France to care for the growing number of Jewish refugee children. The children received mainstream education as well as training in physical education and survival skills, to prepare them for possible future dangers.

In 1941, one of the leaders of the OSE, Madame Andree Salomon, worked with international agencies to secure the emigration of more than 350 Jewish children from southern France to the United States. After the Nazis accelerated their extermination policies with the formulation of the Final Solution in 1942, the OSE established an underground network to smuggle many of the remaining children into neutral countries, such as Switzerland.

In the aftermath of the war, the work of the OSE continued, in particular to disperse the children under its care to homes in France or to other countries, including Palestine and the US.

Over the many decades since, OSE has evolved to meet the changing needs of the community. Today its work focuses on the key areas of child affairs, health, disability and geriatrics. The name Ruth Kneppel can still be found on its honour board of social workers.

Ruth's OSE identity card

REFERENCES

Testimony of Ruth Stein, given to Jewish Holocaust Centre, Melbourne, 2002

American Joint Distribution Committee, Vienna, Austria, 21 May 1946, File 27535

Curriculum Vitae of Ruth Kneppel, France, 1946

Oral history of Curt Kneppel, as told to his son Peter, USA, c. late 1970s

Anne Sebba, *Les Parisiennes*, St Martin's Press, 2016

Danielle Darquié, *Dans les pas des Résistants*, Reprolaser, 2018

IVRIA Recollections, Typed notes distributed at the IVRIA 80th anniversary celebrations, Israel, April 1971

www.ingramcontent.com/pod-product-compliance
Lightning Source LLC
Chambersburg PA
CBHW061405160426
42811CB00114B/2390/J